CITYSPOTS
FRANKFURT

Grant Bourne

Thomas Cook

D0378156

Written by Grant Bourne
Updated by Kate Hairsine

Published by Thomas Cook Publishing
A division of Thomas Cook Tour Operations Limited
Company registration No: 1450464 England
The Thomas Cook Business Park, 9 Coningsby Road
Peterborough PE3 8SB, United Kingdom
Email: sales@thomascook.com, Tel: +44 (0)1733 416477
www.thomascookpublishing.com

Produced by The Content Works Ltd
Aston Court, Kingsmead Business Park, Frederick Place
High Wycombe, Bucks HP11 1LA
www.thecontentworks.com

Series design based on an original concept by Studio 183 Limited

ISBN: 978-1-84157-871-2

First edition © 2006 Thomas Cook Publishing
This second edition © 2008 Thomas Cook Publishing
Text © Thomas Cook Publishing
Maps © Thomas Cook Publishing/PCGraphics (UK) Limited
Transport map © Communicarta Limited

Series Editor: Kelly Anne Pipes
Production/DTP: Steven Collins

Printed and bound in Spain by GraphyCems

Cover photography (Hammering Man) © Grant Faint/Getty Images

CONTENTS

SYMBOLS KEY

The following symbols are used throughout this book:

ⓐ address ☎ telephone 🄵 fax Ⓦ website address
🄻 opening times Ⓝ public transport connections

The following symbols are used on the maps:

🄸 information office		▢	points of interest
✈ airport		○	city
➕ hospital		○	large town
🄿 police station		○	small town
🄱 bus station		═	motorway
🄴 railway station		▬	main road
Ⓤ U-Bahn		▬	minor road
🆂 S-Bahn		──	railway
✝ cathedral			
❶ numbers denote featured cafés & restaurants			

Hotels and restaurants are graded by approximate price as follows:
£ budget price ££ mid-range price £££ expensive

Abbreviations used in addresses:
Str., -str. Strasse, -strasse (street, road)
Pl., -pl. Platz, platz (square)

◗ *The top of the Zeil has great views of Frankfurt's skyline*

INTRODUCING
Frankfurt

Introduction

Frankfurt is a serious city. Its skyscrapers pierce the sky. Its river, the Main, slashes the city brutally in half. Its wide streets are always heaving. Its luxury stores are packed. Its clubs and bars pump out electro-beats. Its opera singers and top orchestras compete. Its bankers, from the 350 banks based here, move and shake the world. Frankfurt is a serious city.

And it's a seriously fun city. What do you want to do? Shop? Head for Goethestrasse or the Zeil, where you can join the crowds in picking up the latest in fashion or design.

You want to eat? You have the whole culinary world to choose from, as well as some of the best traditional German food you'll find for miles.

You fancy some culture? Frankfurt spends more on the performing arts than any other city in Germany. The impressive Alte Oper is the place to hear some the most accomplished classical musicians in the world. Opera and ballet are part of the city's essence.

Or you just want to party? Pick up the edgy music scene in Hauptbahnhof. Electronic, if you can take it, but just about everything else if you can't.

The people of Frankfurt love a good festival, and the calendar's packed. Summer is the time for live rock, pop and jazz in the streets of the city centre. Christmas is a must for Christmas markets, guaranteed. If you can't find what you want, take a photo and give that instead – the Römerberg is a picture-postcard scene you just can't miss.

So what do you do when you can't take the pace of this vibrant, modern city any longer? Hike it off in the nearby forest-covered hills of the Taunus. Drink it off in the vineyards of the Rheingau. Visit the

⬤ *Frankfurt's old and new architecture, seen from the Kaiserdom*

historic cities of Wiesbaden and Mainz and sit in splendid peace in one of Germany's most spectacular cathedrals. Or, if you're the indulgent sort, lie back and dream in one of their luxury spas.

Whoever you are, whatever you want to do, Frankfurt will open up and help you find it.

When to go

There are great things to do throughout the year in Frankfurt. As in most cities, though, it is during summer that Frankfurt really comes alive. The streets are filled non-stop with colourful parades, street festivals and open-air concerts.

Summer is also the best time to explore the surroundings. You'll see some spectacular fireworks displays on the Rhine, drink some unforgettable wine at wine festivals in the Rheingau, and dance and sing at spectacular castle festivals in the Taunus hills.

SEASONS & CLIMATE

The Rhine plains and the Rhein-Main region enjoy mild weather, protected by the hills of the Taunus, Spessart and Odenwald. The Taunus area is higher up, so it is usually cooler. Spring arrives early

● The Palmengarten is a great place to relax on a hot day

in March, with average temperatures around 8°–15°C (46°–59°F). The atmosphere can be quite damp in spring and early autumn, but with the cool temperatures walking and cycling in the area are still a pleasure. Full summer can be hot and muggy, and a good time to enjoy the shade of Frankfurt's many parks. In winter, temperatures in the city seldom drop much below zero, but you can go cross-country skiing in the Taunus hills.

ANNUAL EVENTS

These are just a few of the annual events held in Frankfurt and the Rhein-Main region. Note that exact dates may change from year to year, so do check with the tourist offices first. For a comprehensive calendar of events, see Ⓦ www.frankfurt-tourismus.de

February

Fastnacht (carnival) is celebrated everywhere in the region, but the highlight is the **Rosenmontagszug** in Mainz (4 Feb 2008, 23 Feb 2009). The procession that takes place on the Monday before Lent actually begins on Ash Wednesday.

March–April

Luminale A bi-annual festival (2008, then 2010) held over four days during the city's Light & Building trade fair. Spectacular light displays are combined with sound and performance Ⓦ www.luminale.com

Spring Dippemess Frankfurt's largest folk festival, held over three weeks from mid-March to early April Ⓦ www.dippemess.de

Nacht der Museen (Museums Night) Frankfurt's museums stay open late with a varied programme of events ☏ (069) 9746 0555 Ⓦ www.nacht-der-museen.de

May

Wäldchestag (Forest Day) is a unique folk festival held in the City Forest Sat–Tues of the Whitsun long weekend.
ⓐ Am Oberforsthaus, Frankfurt Stadtwald ⓒ 12.00–01.00
ⓢ S-Bahn: 21; bus: 51, 61 to Oberforsthaus

June

Rosen und Lichterfest (Rose and Light Festival) in the Palmengarten.
ⓦ www.palmengarten-frankfurt.de

Höchster Schlossfest (Castle Festival) A month of exhibitions, theatre and concerts in Höchst from early June to early July.
ⓦ www.vereinsring-hoechst.de

Opernplatzfest A feast of culinary treats and live music on Opernplatz, between late June and early July.
ⓦ www.opernplatzfest.de

Parade der Kulturen (Parade of Cultures) celebrates Frankfurt's multicultural character with a colourful parade through the inner city.
ⓦ www.parade-der-kulturen.de

July–August

Museumsuferfest (Museum Embankment Festival) brings both banks of the Main alive at the end of August with music, theatre and more. ⓦ www.museumsuferfest-frankfurt.de

September

IAA (International Motor Show), held every two years. Next in 2009.
ⓦ www.iaa.de

Autumn Dippemess Folk festival lasting one week.
ⓦ www.dippemess.de

October
Buchmesse (Book Fair) is the world's most important book-publishing trade fair, held over six days in early October. Open to the public at the weekend. Ⓦ www.buchmesse.de
Eurocity Marathon takes place in late October, with accompanying street festivals. Ⓦ www.frankfurt-marathon.com

November–December
Frankfurter Weihnachtsmarkt (Christmas Market), on the Römerberg, Paulspl. and Mainkai, from end November until Christmas.

PUBLIC HOLIDAYS
New Year's Day 1 Jan
Good Friday 21 March 2008, 10 Apr 2009
Easter Monday 24 March 2008, 12 Apr 2009
Labour Day 1 May
Ascension Day 1 May 2008, 21 May 2009
Whit Monday 12 May 2008, 1 June 2009
Corpus Christi 22 May 2008, 11 June 2009
German Unification Day 3 Oct
Christmas 25 and 26 Dec

Many shops and businesses also close in the afternoon on the following days: Thursday before Rose Monday, Rose Monday, *Wälchestag* (Tuesday after Whit Monday), Christmas Eve and New Year's Eve.

Reaching for the sky

Frankfurt's skyline is dominated by skyscrapers. The glistening glass towers have earned it the nickname 'Mainhattan', a play on the river Main, which runs through the city.

More than 80 per cent of Frankfurt was destroyed in World War II bombing and the historic centre was completely flattened. When the Frankfurthers rebuilt during Germany's economic boom in the 1960s and 1970s, they looked upwards.

Most of Frankfurt's skyscrapers are concentrated in the so-called *Bankersviertel* (bank district) between the Alte Oper and the main railway station. There you'll find the Commerzbank-Tower, Europe's second tallest building at 300 m (984 ft), counting the mast at the top. It was not only the tallest building in Europe when it was built in 1997, but one of the greenest due to its nine gardens and energy-saving technologies.

Probably Frankfurt's best known building is its second tallest at 257 m (842 ft), the Messeturm in the city's Westend. With its distinctive pyramid design crowning a slim tower, the Messeturm is nicknamed the *Bleistift* (pencil) by locals.

Not far from the Messeturm is Frankfurt's third tallest high-rise at 208 m (682 ft), the Westendstrasse Tower. The building has a distinctive crown, which is heated in winter to stop icicles dropping on people 53 storeys below.

The Japan Centre in the finance district is smaller at 115 m (377 ft), but architecturally interesting. The red granite building has a characteristic Japanese design and overhanging roof, with a Japanese stone garden in the front.

One of Frankfurt's most modest but beautiful skyscrapers is the Main Plaza hotel in Sachsenhausen. At only 88 m (289 ft), it was inspired by the 1920s American Radiator Building in midtown New York.

Most of the skyscrapers are office blocks and banks, so inaccessible to the public. The Maintower offers the most spectacular bird's eye view on the city from 200 m (656 ft) for a charge. A great free view of the skyline can be had from the top floor of the Zeilgalerie shopping centre, which is connected to the rooftop terrace of the Galeria Kaufhof department store.

Main Turm (Main Tower) ❸ Neue Mainzer Str. 52–58
ⓦ www.maintower.helaba.de ⓛ Viewing platform 10.00–21.00 Sun–Thur, 10.00–23.00 Fri & Sat (summer); 10.00–19.00 Sun–Thur, 10.00–21.00 Fri & Sat (winter); closed in bad weather ⓢ S-Bahn: 19 to Taunusanlage; U-Bahn: 6, 7 to Alte Oper. Admission charge

🔺 *Watch the clouds pass In Frankfurt's urban towers*

History

Frankfurt has over a thousand years of recorded history, but there are traces of settlement from around 3,000 BC on Cathedral Hill, between Römer and the cathedral. The Romans were here in the first century AD, and it was the Franks around 500 AD, who gave the city its name, which means 'Ford of the Franks'.

The 8th century Frankish Emperor Charlemagne set the ball rolling for Frankfurt's further rise when he made Franconovurd, as it was then known, one of his royal residences. By the 12th century the market town was already attracting traders and merchants from far and wide, and in 1147 Frankfurt became the permanent site of the election and crowning of the German kings and later Holy Roman Emperors (see below). In 1372 the city achieved virtual autonomy from the *Kaiser* (Emperor) and was able to control its own finances.

Frankfurt's steady rise to wealth and importance was not without the occasional hiccup. During the 16th-century Reformation Frankfurt's citizens embraced the Protestant teachings of Martin Luther, but were forced to reverse their ban on Catholic services after the Catholics under Kaiser Karl V soundly defeated their Protestant rivals in the Schmalkald War of 1546–7. Frankfurt was occupied by Swedish troops in the 17th century during the Thirty Years War, then repeatedly by the French in the 18th and early 19th centuries. In 1848 the German National Assembly met briefly at St Paul's Church in Frankfurt, in an early but ultimately unsuccessful attempt to set up a democratic constitution in Germany.

The basis for Frankfurt's present status as one of the world's great financial centres was laid back in the 16th century by business-minded Dutch refugees – the year 1585 marked the birth of Frankfurt's stock

HOLY ROMAN EMPERORS

Arising from the eastern part of Charlemagne's empire in the 9th century, the Holy Roman Empire (HRE) saw itself as the successor to the Roman Empire of antiquity. It existed for nearly a millennium, from the Middle Ages until the early 19th century. At the height of its power, it comprised much of Western and Central Europe, centred on Germany and Austria. However, the HRE never became a nation state like France, as attempts to set up a strong central government failed. Napoleon dissolved it in 1806 after his victory against Russia and Austria at Austerlitz. The Emperors, or Kaisers, of the HRE are not to be confused with the Kaisers of the German Empire, which was founded in 1870 and ended with the defeat of Kaiser Wilhelm II at the end of World War I.

exchange. Later, in the 18th and 19th centuries, it was the city's oft-maligned Jewish citizens who cemented the city's reputation as an international banking metropolis. Their influence on the business, cultural and academic life of Frankfurt came to a tragic end with the Nazi pogroms in 1938. In March 1944 Allied bombers completely destroyed the city centre.

Though Frankfurt narrowly lost out to Bonn in becoming capital of West Germany in 1949, it is Germany's undisputed financial and business capital. The European Central Bank and Europe's largest trade fair centre are based here, cementing its reputation as a commercial hub. But culture is as big as business here. Today's skyscrapers may be the symbols of modern Frankfurt, but the restored Römer displays the city's bonds to an equally illustrious past.

Lifestyle

Frankfurt is a cosmopolitan city. Thousands of foreigners come and go every day, and many stay. Over 180 nationalities live and work in Frankfurt, more than a quarter of whom don't carry a German passport. This, and the fact that the city has been for centuries a trading centre of European importance, has helped make its citizens tolerant and open to new ideas.

Frankfurt is also a job magnet. Nearly 300,000 commuters pour into the city every day. But it's not all work and no play. The locals also know how to celebrate.

Throughout the year there are dozens of festivals and events. Young businessmen and -women fill the 'after work' parties in the city's many discos and clubs. Restaurants and pubs are packed in the evenings, and bankers rub shoulders with tradesmen in Sachsenhausen's *Ebbelwei* (apple wine) taverns. In summer, office workers sit at outdoor cafés, soaking up a bit of sunshine before returning to the grind.

Frankfurt is very much an outdoor city. Every week in summer thousands of skaters fill the streets on Skate Night (see page 33), or flock to parks along the Main to jog, picnic or relax. Distances are short, and walking or cycling is the usual form of transport for locals.

Compared to a city like London, the cost of living is not too steep. Although housing can be expensive in the inner-city districts and in outlying towns with good public transport connections, visitors holidaying in Frankfurt will find it cheaper than other big cities such as London, Rome or Madrid.

● *The city at dusk*

Culture

The statistics are impressive: Frankfurt has nearly 60 museums, over 30 theatres and more than 100 galleries. And it's not just quantity, it's quality.

The Frankfurt Opera Company is one of the best in Germany. The William Forsythe Company is internationally renowned for its performances of modern ballet. The Senckenberg Museum of natural history (see page 97) is the largest and most important of its kind in Germany.

Collecting has long been a passion of the city's prosperous citizens, and numerous museum collections date from the 18th or early 19th centuries. Many of Frankfurt's best museums line the Schaumainkai (see page 81), which is also known as the *Museumsufer* (Museum Embankment). Within easy walking distance, you can admire sculptures from ancient Greece and Rome, watch classic films (often in the original language) in a museum for cinematic art, learn about the birth of the Information Age and view masterworks by such artists as Jan van Eyck and Renoir.

Cultural highlights not to be missed are the Nacht der Museen in April and Museumsuferfest in August (see pages 9 and 10). On these occasions you can enjoy an exciting programme of events centred around the city's cultural institutions.

There are also numerous private collections worth a visit. Around the Kunsthalle Schirn, the Museum of Modern Art and the Kunstverein, you'll find a lively gallery scene, where you can also buy works of art. Try **Artbox** (ⓐ Braubachstr. 37 ⓣ (069) 2193 5555), **Frankfurter Kunstkabinett** (ⓐ Braubachstr. 14–16 ⓣ (069) 281 085 ⓦ www.frankfurter-kunstkabinett.de) and **Galerie Schuster** (ⓐ Fahrgasse 8 ⓣ (069) 292 993 ⓦ www.galerie-schuster.de).

The performing arts are also alive and well in Frankfurt. Schauspiel's theatrical productions and local opera and ballet companies show a willingness to experiment, and these avant-garde productions are well balanced with more traditional performances.

Most performances are in German, but you can try the **English Theatre** (ⓐ Kaiserstr. 34 ① (069) 242 31620 Ⓦ www.english-theatre.org) for English-language comedies, musicals and serious plays. The **Internationales Theater** (ⓐ Hanauer Landstr. 5–7 ① (069) 499 0980 Ⓦ www.internationales-theater.de) also occasionally puts on works in English and other European languages.

◗ *Check out the Kunsthalle Schirn while you're in the Altstadt*

Also popular and, and great fun, are the various folk, cabaret and variety theatres dotted about the city.

Classical music is another big part of Frankfurt's cultural life. The hr-Sinfonieorchester is world class, as are the Museumsorchester, the Ensemble Modern and the Mutare-Ensemble. As well as the city's own orchestras, there are regular guest performances by renowned orchestras and musicians from around the world.

If you are after something more noisy, Frankfurt is the capital of techno music. Live performances of rock, pop and jazz are also put on in a number of excellent clubs and venues like the Alte Oper. In summer there are regular open-air performances.

ADMISSION CHARGES & OPENING HOURS

All museums charge an admission fee unless otherwise stated. Municipal museums are free on Wednesdays. The Museumsufer ticket offers discounted admission to 25 institutions. Entrance to churches is free, though their attached museums have a charge. Most galleries and museums are closed on Mondays but open on public holidays, even if this is a Monday. They are closed at Christmas and on New Year's Day. Public holiday opening hours are the same as for Sundays.

▶ *View of Frankfurt from across the Main*

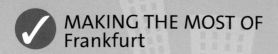

Shopping

The city is filled with luxury stores such as Tiffany's and Chanel, and foreign-language bookshops and other specialist stores cater for the large foreign population. You don't have to go far in the inner city to find what you want, as trendy fashion boutiques rub shoulders with second-hand shops, and open-air markets are close to modern shopping passages. And to make your shopping experience complete, there is an excellent choice of cafés.

Most of the city's more exclusive shops are between Rossmarkt and the Alte Oper. In Goethestrasse, Frankfurt's modest version of New York's Fifth Avenue, you'll find names such as Armani, Chanel, Tiffany and Gucci. Other luxury shops are in Steinweg, Schillerstrasse and Fressgasse (Grosse Bockenheimer Strasse). The latter is especially good if you are looking for gourmet foods and top-quality wines.

More down to earth are the shops and department stores flanking the Zeil, Frankurt's main shopping drag.

Competition is strong, and there is regular price-slashing around mid-summer and in December. You can pick up good bargains at the city's most well-known flea market, on Saturday mornings along Schaumainkai.

If you are looking for souvenirs consider buying a *Bembel*, a glazed stoneware jug used for serving Frankfurt's traditional drink, apple wine. Sachsenhausen is the place to find it.

Germany has recently deregulated its shopping hours, so while many stores and supermarkets in Frankfurt close at 20.00 some of the bigger chains are now extending their opening times. With few exceptions, all stores are closed on Sundays.

USEFUL SHOPPING PHRASES

What time do the shops open/close?
Um wieviel Uhr öffnen/schliessen die Geschäfte?
Oom veefeel oor erffnen/shleessen dee geshefter?

How much is this?
Wieviel kostet das?
Veefeel kostet dass?

Can I try this on?
Kann ich das anprobieren?
Can ikh dass anprobeeren?

My size is ...
Ich habe Grösse ...
Ikh haber grerser ...

I'll take this one, thank you
Ich nehme das, danke schön
Ikh neymer dass, danker shern

Can you show me the one in the window/this one?
Zeigen Sie mir bitte das im Fenster/dieses da?
Tsyegen zee mere bitter dass im fenster/deezess dar?

Eating & drinking

Frankfurt boasts a huge range of cafés and restaurants catering to all tastes and pockets. The choice of food styles reflects the international mix of people who live here. For traditional Frankfurter fare, the *Ebbelwei* (apple wine) taverns are the best bet. If cooking for yourself, visit the local food markets and food sections of the large department stores.

Many restaurants are open for lunch between 12.00 and 15.00, and for dinner from 17.00 or 18.00 until late. For breakfast or brunch, head for one of the city's numerous cafés. Around the railway station they often open by 07.00 or earlier, and elsewhere in town from 08.00. A restaurant's *Ruhetag* (day off) is displayed by the door along with the menu.

Look out for the bargain-priced *Mittagstisch* (lunchtime set menu). Any establishment advertising *Gutbürgerliche Küche* (simple home-style cooking) are generally good value, and normally have a *Stammtisch*, a table reserved for regular customers.

Vegetarians will find plenty of non-meat dishes at Indian, Chinese or Thai restaurants, and many cafés offer large mixed salads as a main dish. For fully vegetarian restaurants, try **Naturbar** (£ ⓐ Oeder Weg 26 ❶ (069) 554 486 ⓦ www.naturbarfrankfurt.de ❻ 11.30–15.30, 18.00–23.00 Mon–Fri, 18.00–23.00 Sat, closed Sun ⓝ U-Bahn: 1–3 to Eschenheimer Tor) or **Arche Nova** (££ ⓐ Kasseler

---

PRICE CATEGORIES

Based on the average price of a main dish without drinks.

£ up to €10   ££ €10–€20   £££ above €20

Str. 1a ☎ (069) 97785661 ⏱ 12.00–01.00 Mon–Sat (kitchen closes 23.30), 10.00–17.00 Sun ⓦ www.arche-nova.de Ⓢ S-Bahn: 3–6 to Frankfurt West). The Turkish Tandure (see page 88) also has a large selection of vegetarian dishes.

There is a kosher restaurant, **Sohar**, in the Jewish Community Centre in the Westend (ⓦ www.sohars-restaurant.de ⏱ 12.00–19.00 Tues–Thur, 12.00–16.00 Sun, Fridays phone to ask Ⓤ U-Bahn: 6, 7 to Westend).

Formal dress is rarely required in German restaurants, except perhaps for evening dining at a few top locations. Unless you go to a more upmarket restaurant, it's usually okay to just seat yourself

🔺 *If it is sausages you're looking for, start at the Kleinmarkthalle*

EBBELWEI TAVERNS

Frankfurt's *Ebbelwei* taverns are good places to eat local specialities. Try eggs and potatoes with *Frankfurter Grüne Sosse* (green herb sauce), *Frankfurter Rippchen* (pickled pork ribs) served with *sauerkraut* (pickled cabbage), or *Handkäs mit Musik*. The latter is a round curd cheese marinated in vinaigrette and served with onions, and the music is a reference to the subsequent noisy digestion process. The famous frankfurter sausage often appears on local menus as a snack, or as a main dish served with sauerkraut or potatoes. This smoked pork sausage has been around for over 500 years, and only sausage-makers from the Frankfurt region have the right to sell their product as *Frankfurter Würstchen*.

at any empty table. Tipping is not a must, but customary for good service. Small sums are rounded off, larger amounts (over €30) might include a tip of around 5 per cent.

The locals enjoy a glass of wine or mug of beer as much as they appreciate eating out. Most cafés and all restaurants serve alcoholic beverages, and those places normally associated with just beer or wine, such as *Weinstuben* (wine bars) or *Biergärten* (beer gardens), also offer at least simple meals. Frankfurt's traditional drink, *Ebbelwei*, a sour-tasting apple wine or cider, is best enjoyed in the taverns of Sachsenhausen.

Coffee is the most popular non-alcoholic drink, but virtually all cafés and restaurants serve both herbal and black teas. Bottled

● *Try a traditional apple wine tavern with a jug of* Ebbelwei

Stilles (still water) or *Sprudelwasser* (sparkling water) are widely available. Kids might enjoy an *Apfelschörle* (apple juice mixed with *Sprudelwasser*) as a healthier alternative to fizzy drinks.

The city, with its many parks, provides ample scope for picnicking. Near the inner city try Bethmann Park and the Nizza Anlage (Nizza Garden, see page 62). In Sachsenhausen there are green spaces right next to the river along Shaumainkai. In Westend, Grüneburgpark (see page 92) provides plenty of room for a picnic.

Among the best places to look for food supplies are the weekly food markets. A good choice is the Kaiserstrasse Wochenmarkt, not far from the main railway station, or those along Schillerstrasse and at Konstablerwache. Open throughout the week and conveniently close to the city's old quarter is the Kleinmarkthalle, a covered market. On the Zeil, both Karstadt and Galeria Kaufhof have excellent food sections. Gourmet take-aways are available from the delicatessens along Fressgasse.

USEFUL DINING PHRASES

I would like a table for ... people
Ein Tisch für ... Personen, bitte
Ine teesh foor ... perzohnen, bitter

Waiter/waitress!
Herr Ober/Fräulein, bitte!
Hair ohber/froyline, bitter!

May I have the bill, please?
Die Rechnung, bitte?
Dee rekhnung, bitter?

Could I have it well-cooked/medium/rare please?

Ich möchte es bitte durch/halb durch/englisch gebraten?

Ikh merkhter es bitter doorkh/halb doorkh/eng-lish gebrarten?

I am a vegetarian. Does this contain meat?

Ich bin Vegetarier (Vegetarierin fem.). Enthält das hier Fleisch?

Ish bin veggetaareer (veggetaareerin). Enthelt dass heer flyshe?

Where is the toilet (restroom) please?

Wo sind die Toiletten, bitte?

Voo zeent dee toletten, bitter?

I would like a cup of/two cups of/another coffee/tea, please

Ich möchte eine Tasse/zwei Tassen/noch eine Tasse Kaffee/
Tee, bitte

*Ikh merkhter iner tasser/tsvy tassen/nokh iner tasser kafey/
tey, bitter*

I would like a beer/two beers, please

Ein Bier/Zwei Biere, bitte

Ine beer/tsvy beerer, bitter

Entertainment & nightlife

Cool jazz clubs, even cooler discos, transvestite shows and philharmonic concerts, gay bars and blues bars, opera and cabaret: the possibilities for a night on the town are limited only by one's wallet or stamina. In summer, open-air events draw the crowds into town.

The city's pub and bar scene is colourful and varied. From some you can enjoy fantastic views over Frankfurt's skyline, in others television screens keep you informed on the stock market or the latest soccer scores. Background music ranges from bar piano to jazz and electronic sounds – many bars have regular live music in the evenings.

Those looking for a glass of wine in a relaxing atmosphere should head for one of the city's *Weinstuben* (wine bars). Stick to the inner-city area, as distances are short and the concentration of watering holes is good. Sachsenhausen is also a good choice, especially around the area of Altsachsenhausen. Here you'll also find a good selection of Irish pubs.

It's not always easy to distinguish the city's bar scene from its clubs and discos. In many cases you'll find an establishment is bar, dance locale and even restaurant all rolled into one. In any case, there are plenty of flash places to choose from, with techno sounds dominating the dance floors. Most clubs and discos charge for entrance, though a few are free. Some of the best dance venues are around the main railway station and the Hauptwache, otherwise head for the eastern district of Ostend.

Throughout the year there are regular rock, pop and jazz concerts by national and international stars. In summer, concerts are staged in the inner city on Opernplatz. Good, regular live music venues include Batschkapp in Eschersheim, Jazzkeller Frankfurt (see page 73) and the Sinkkasten. Open-air concerts worth noting are Jazz in Palmengarten (June–Sept) and the Sound of Frankfurt (July).

Fans of ballet, opera, classical music and theatre will also find Frankfurt richly endowed. Big classical concerts take place at the Alte Oper (see page 75), while opera and drama are centred around the Städtische Bühnen on Willy-Brandt-Platz. The Bockenheimer Depot, home of the renowned William Forsythe Company, is the place to go for ambitious modern ballet. See the Culture section, pages 18–19, for more information on classical music and the performing arts.

As for cinema, the choice ranges from establishments showing the typical Hollywood blockbusters to small art-house cinemas with more ambitious films. Most films are dubbed in German, though a few are shown in the original language with subtitles. Current English-language films are shown at the **Turm-Palast** (ⓐ Bleichstr. 57 ⓣ (069) 281 787 ⓤ U-Bahn:1–3 to Eschenheimer Tor).

Information on current events and entertainment can be found in the *Frankfurter Woche*, free from tourist offices. More comprehensive listings (in German) are in the *Frankfurter Journal* and the weekly listings supplement 'Plan F' in the *Frankfurter Rundschau* newspaper. See also ⓦ www.frankfurt-rhein-main.de

For tickets, ask at the local tourist office or visit Best Tickets ⓐ Zeil 112. The ticket and information hotline Frankfurt Ticket (ⓐ Hauptwache-Passage (next to Kaufhof department store) ⓣ (069) 134 0400 ⓦ www.frankfurt-ticket.de ⓛ 09.30–19.00 Mon–Fri, 09.30–16.00 Sat ⓤ U-Bahn: Hauptwache) sells most theatre, opera, ballet and concert tickets.

Sport & relaxation

Frankfurt claims to be the sports capital of Germany a claim that is not unjustified. The city's ice hockey and basketball teams have both been national champions, the American football team is a top contender in the European League and the women's soccer team belongs to the world's best. Frankfurt also has an excellent sport infrastructure, and there are plenty of possibilities for visitors to enjoy sport themselves.

SPECTATOR SPORTS
For tickets to important games and events contact Frankfurt Ticket (page 31).

American Football The local team is Frankfurt Galaxy and you can watch them play at the Commerzbank-Arena (Waldstadion). ⓐ Frankfurter Waldstadion, Mörfelder Landstr. 362 ⓦ www.frankfurt-galaxy.de ⓝ S-Bahn: 8, 9 to Sportfeld

Football (Soccer) Important games are played at the Commerzbank-Arena (Waldstadion). ⓐ Frankfurter Waldstadion, Mörfelder Landstr. 362 ⓝ S-Bahn: 8, 9 to Sportfeld

Ice Hockey The Frankfurt Lions are the local team. Catch their games at the Eissporthalle. ⓐ Am Bornheimer Hang 4 ⓦ www.frankfurt-lions.de ⓝ U-Bahn: 7 to Eissporthalle

Rugby SC Frankfurt 1880 founded Germany's first professional rugby team in 2006. ⓐ Feldgerichtstr. 29 ⓦ www.sc1880.de/rugby ⓝ U-Bahn:1–3 to Dornbusch then 15 minutes walk

PARTICIPATION SPORTS

Cycling, Jogging, Walking Grüneburgpark or the banks of the Main are good spots for these activities. For longer tours head for the Taunus hills (see page 106). *Wanderkarten* and *Radwanderkarten* (walking and cycling maps) are available from bookshops.

Call-A-Bike (bike hire) ❶ 0700 0522 5522 Ⓦ www.callabike-interaktiv.de

Eissporthalle Frankfurt Indoor and outdoor ice-skating rinks. Skates for hire. Closed mid-Apr–Sept. ❸ Am Bornheimer Hang 4, Bornheim ❶ (069) 2123 9308 Ⓦ www.eissporthalle-frankfurt.de Ⓝ U-Bahn: 7; S-Bahn: 12 to Eissporthalle

Swimming Ask at the tourist office for a list of indoor and outdoor pools, or check www.bbf-frankfurt.de. One of the best is **Panorama Bad**, which also has a sauna. ❸ Inheidener Str. 60 ❶ (069) 462 340 Ⓝ U-Bahn: 7 to Eissporthalle; S-Bahn: 14 to Ernst-May-Pl.

Tuesday Night Skating On these nights you can skate along a 40 km (85 miles) route closed to traffic. ❸ Deutschherrenufer near the Ignaz-Bubis-Brücke ❶ (069) 622 703 Ⓦ www.t-n-s.de ❸ From 20.30 Tues, Mar–Oct

Skaters World Rollerblade hire ❸ Hamburger Allee 65 ❶ (069) 777 307 Ⓦ www.skatersworld.de ❸ 10.00–13.00, 14.00–19.00 Mon–Fri, 10.00–14.00 Sat Ⓝ S-Bahn: 3–6 to Westbahnhof

Accommodation

Frankfurt cannot offer much cheap accommodation near the city centre, since most visitors are here on business. However, more hotels are now catering to independent travellers, and prices can drop at weekends. Some hotels offer attractive weekend packages for particular events or dinner and opera trips.

Most hotels are around the *Hauptbahnhof* (central railway station) and inner city, though it is worth looking in Bockenheim, Westend, Nordend, Ostend and Sachsenhausen.

Around the Trade Fair grounds and the inner-city area are most of the upper-price hotels and a few in the mid-price range (3-star).

Cheaper accommodation can be found at a *Gasthaus*, *Pension* or *Privatzimmer*, which are roughly equivalent to B&Bs.

A couple of camping grounds are located on the city's outskirts, and there is a youth hostel in the district of Sachsenhausen. Generally, the further from the inner city you are, the cheaper it gets.

It pays to book well ahead for accommodation, especially during major trade fairs when hotel prices shoot up.

For advance bookings of hotels try the Congress and Tourist Centre's website at ⓦ www.frankfurt-tourismus.de. For cheaper

PRICE CATEGORIES

Hotels in Germany are graded according to a voluntary 1- to 5-star rating system, which conforms to international standards. The ratings in this book are as follows:

£ up to €99 ££ €100–€199 £££ over €200, based on a single night in a double room for two people.

accommodation try Ⓦ www.bedandbreakfast.de, Ⓦ www.frankfurt-pension.de, Ⓦ www.bandb-ring.de and Ⓦ www.pension.de

HOTELS & GUEST HOUSES

Artroom-f £ Small artist-run *pension* between the railway station and the river. ⓐ Werftstr. 16, Gutleutviertel ⓣ (069) 343 545 or (0173) 814 2310 Ⓦ www.artroom-f.de Ⓝ U-Bahn/S-Bahn: Frankfurt Hbf

Hotelschiff Peter Schlott £ Sleep on an old boat on the Main River. The cabins are small, but spotlessly clean and well-priced. ⓐ Batterie (Höchst Mainufer), Frankfurt Höchst. ⓣ (069) 3004 643 Ⓦ www.hotelschiffschlott.de Ⓝ S-Bahn: Höchst

Pension Aller £ Charming art deco *pension* with light and airy rooms, close to railway station and downtown. ⓐ Gutleutstr. 94 ⓣ (069) 252 596 ⓕ (069) 232 330 Ⓦ www.pension-aller.de Ⓝ U-Bahn/S-Bahn: Frankfurt Hbf

Pension Geoyes City £ Heated with geothermal energy, high-speed internet in all rooms. ⓐ Heisterstr. 28, Sachsenhausen ⓣ (069) 6032 60060 ⓕ 6032 60032 Ⓦ www.pension-geoyes.de Ⓝ S-Bahn: Lokalbahnhof

Waldhotel Hensel's Felsenkeller £ Modest family hotel 15-min tram ride from the centre, on the edge of the city's forest Restaurant ⓐ Buchrainstr. 95, Frankfurt-Oberrad ⓣ (069) 652 086 Ⓦ www.waldhotel-frankfurt.de Ⓝ Tram: Buchrainstrasse

Hotel am Berg £–££ Palatial old villa with spacious rooms. ⓐ Grethenweg 23, Sachsenhausen ⓣ (069) 660 5370

🕿 (069) 615 109 🌐 www.hotel-am-berg-ffm.de Ⓜ U-Bahn/S-Bahn:
Frankfurt Süd

Hotel Gölz £–££ Attractive villa with spacious rooms and good
breakfast buffet. 🏠 Beethovenstr. 44, Westend 🕿 (069) 746 735
🖷 746 142 🌐 www.hotel-goelz.de Ⓜ U-Bahn: Westend

A Casa ££ Handy for sights like the Senckenbergmuseum.
🏠 Varrentrappstr. 49, Bockenheim 🕿 (069) 9798 8821 🖷 (069) 9798 8822
🌐 www.hotel-acasa.de Ⓜ U-Bahn: Bockenheimer Warte

Alexander am Zoo ££ Next to Frankfurt's zoo, 15 min walk
to the Konstablerwache. Generous buffet breakfast.
🏠 Waldschmidtstr. 59–61, Ostend 🕿 (069) 949 600
🖷 (069) 9496 0720 🌐 www.alexanderamzoo.de Ⓜ U-Bahn: Zoo

Bristol Hotel ££ Chic hotel with internet in all rooms. Near Trade
Fair grounds and railway station. 🏠 Ludwigstr. 15, Bahnhofsviertel
🕿 (069) 242 390 🖷 (069) 251 539 🌐 www.bristol-hotel.de
Ⓜ U-Bahn/S-Bahn: Frankfurt Hbf

Hotel am Dom ££ Quiet accommodation in Frankfurt's old quarter,
right behind the cathedral. 🏠 Kannengiessergasse 3, City 🕿 (069) 282 141
🖷 (069) 283 237 🌐 www.hotelamdom.de Ⓜ U-Bahn: Dom/Römer

Hotel Kautz ££ Pleasant, reasonably priced hotel close to the
Museumsufer and picturesque quarter of Altsachsenhausen.
🏠 Gartenstr. 17, Sachsenhausen 🕿 (069) 618 061 🖷 (069) 213 236
🌐 www.hotelkautz.de Ⓜ U-Bahn: Schweizer Platz

Hotel Liebig ££ Small but comfortable family-run hotel in Frankfurt's Westend, near the Palmengarten and Grüneburgpark. ⓐ Liebigstr. 45 ⓣ (069) 2418 2990 ⓦ www.hotelliebig.de ⓝ U-Bahn: Westend or Grüneburgweg

Hotel Nizza ££ Charming, tastefully furnished hotel near the railway station. Good views from the rooftop garden. ⓐ Elbestr. 10, Bahnhofsviertel ⓣ (069) 242 5380 ⓕ 2425 3830 ⓦ www.hotelnizza.de ⓝ U-Bahn/S-Bahn: Frankfurt Hbf

● *Enjoy a drink in the stylish bar at the Bristol Hotel*

Hotel Beethoven ££–£££ Lovely Westend villa with all comforts.
🅰 Beethovenstr. 46, Westend 📞 (069) 743 4970 📠 (069) 748 466
🌐 www.hotelbeethoven.de Ⓝ U-Bahn: Westend

Frankfurter Hof £££ The grandest of Frankfurt's grand hotels with all the
luxury you might expect. 🅰 Am Kaiserpl., City 📞 (069) 215 02 📠 215 900
🌐 www.frankfurter-hof.steigenberger.de Ⓝ U-Bahn: Dom/Römer

HOSTELS & CAMPSITES

Campingplatz Mainkur £ Around 10 km (6 miles) east of the
city on the River Main, 1 km to the nearest S-Bahn and tram stop
🅰 Frankfurter Landstr. 107, Maintal Dörnigheim 📞 (06109) 412 193
📠 (06109) 65 364 🌐 www.campingplatz-mainkur.de
🕐 mid-Apr–Sept Ⓝ Tram: Frankfurt-Mainkur, then 1km walk

City Camp Frankfurt £ On the River Nidda, with quick U-Bahn
connections into the city. 🅰 An der Samdelmühle 35 📞 (069) 570 332
📠 5700 3604 🌐 www.city-camp-frankfurt.de 🕐 Tent sites from
mid-Apr–Sept only; camper vans and caravan sites all year round.
Ⓝ S-Bahn: Frankfurt-Eschersheim

Frankfurt Hostel £ Clean rooms, internet café and handy for all the sights.
🅰 Kaiserstr. 74, Bahnhofsviertel 📞 (069) 247 5130 📠 (069) 2475 1311
🌐 www.frankfurt-hostel.com Ⓝ U-Bahn/S-Bahn: Frankfurt Hbf

Haus der Jugend (Youth Hostel) **£** Dorms, singles, doubles and even
apartments. Youth Hostel Association or Hostelling International
membership card required. 🅰 Deutschherrnufer 12, Sachsenhausen
📞 (069) 610 0150 📠 (069) 6100 1599 🌐 www.jugendherberge-
frankfurt.de Ⓝ S-Bahn: Schweizer Platz

🔺 The Frankfurter Hof is in the top echelon of the city's hotels

THE BEST OF FRANKFURT

Flying visits to Frankfurt are ideal, as the main attractions are close together in the lively city centre. If you have more time and energy, the surrounding Taunus hills are perfect for walking and cycling.

TOP 10 ATTRACTIONS

- **Römerberg** Frankfurt at its most picturesque (see page 64).

- **Kaiserdom (Imperial Cathedral)** Where German kings and emperors were crowned (see page 62).

- **Palmengarten** One of the world's oldest collections of exotic plants (see ppages 94–6).

- **Boat trips on the Main and Rhine** Discover the city and surrounding countryside from a boat (see pages 78–80 and 117–18).

- **Senckenberg Museum** Dinosaurs and other fascinating exhibits relating to our natural world (see page 97).

- **Städelsches Kunstinstitut (Städel) (City Art Institute)** Artistic masterworks in one of Germany's top museums (see page 83).

- **Festivals** Throughout the year, but above all in summer. The Museumsuferfest and the Christmas Market are a couple of highlights (see pages 10–11).

- **Sachsenhausen** Apple wine taverns and pubs contrast with the polished skyscrapers across the river (see page 76).

- **Skyline** You can't miss it, but don't miss being part of it by visiting the Main Tower (see page 13).

- **Skate Night** On Tuesday nights you can skate with thousands of others through the city (see page 33).

The Städel is a treasure trove of artistic masterpieces

Suggested itineraries

HALF-DAY: FRANKFURT IN A HURRY

Stick to the inner-city area between the Zeil and Römerberg. Begin
on the Römerberg, then head over to the cathedral a few minutes
away. Follow Domstrasse past the Museum of Modern Art to the
Kleinmarkthalle, a lively covered market Pop to the top of the
Zeilgalerie for great views of the skyline. Nearby is the Alte Oper
and Fressgasse, with plenty of choice for coffee and a bite to eat.
On your way back to the Römerberg don't miss the baroque
Hauptwache and Paulskirche.

ONE DAY: TIME TO SEE A LITTLE MORE

Add a museum or two from the Museumsufer (Museum Embankment).
Natural history fans and kids will love the Senckenberg Museum.
The Palmengarten is perfect for all things botanical. Allow time for
shopping along the Zeil or Goethestrasse. In the evening head to an
Ebbelwei (apple wine) tavern in Sachsenhausen.

2–3 DAYS: TIME TO SEE MUCH MORE

Save some time for live music at the famous Jazzkeller, or dance the
night away at one of the city's many discos. Or hear a concert at the
Alte Oper. You could take a cycle trip – ask at the tourist office – or a day
trip to the outlying areas. The Taunus hills and historic cities of Mainz
and Wiesbaden, or a scenic boat trip into the Rheingau are all rewarding.

LONGER: ENJOYING FRANKFURT TO THE FULL

When you're full to the brim of the city's sights and nightlife, spend
a bit more time exploring the surroundings. Consider spending
a few nights in the Taunus, Rheingau or Wiesbaden and Mainz.

● The restored Römer complex in the heart of the city

Something for nothing

It's easy to spend cash in a city like Frankfurt, but you don't have to. The very fact that many of the city's main attractions are located within a compact area means that you can often dispense with public transport and walk. Summer is full of free events, including parades and concerts. So you can have a great time in Frankfurt even on a tight budget.

Thrifty culture freaks should make sure they are in town on Wednesdays, as on this day all the city's municipal museums are free of charge. Museums that are always free include the Frankfurter Apfelweinmuseum (Apple Wine Museum) on the Römerberg and the Museum für Kommunikation (see page 83).

Frankfurt on foot is not only free, but the best way to see the sights. Walking from the main railway station to the Zeil, the city's main shopping street, takes around 15 minutes. From there to the picturesque Römerberg, it is no more than 5 minutes. There is a very pleasant stroll through the shady Nizza Anlage park along the river Main, not far from the Römer. If you then cross the Holbeinsteg, you'll arrive on the Schaumainkai with all its museums. So don't forget to do this on a Wednesday.

Continue through the riverside park to the Eiserner Steg and cross the river back to the Römer. You will have covered much of what there is to see in the inner city, and can still afford a beer on top.

Those with cash in their pockets pay for the views from the Main Tower skyscraper, and those with holes in them ride the elevators to the top of the Zeilgalerie for a free panorama. Other free views of the skyline are from the Sachsenhausen side of the river.

For skating fans on a budget, don't miss the free Tuesday Night Skating sessions (see page 33).

🔺 *The Museumsufer is free on Wednesdays*

When it rains

If it rains while you're in Frankfurt, great. You'll get the chance to explore some of the most fascinating museums and art galleries in Germany, which you might not have done otherwise. Major museums like the Städel (see page 83) shouldn't be missed. Fun for kids and those with an interest in science is the Explora museum (see page 65) with its interactive exhibits. The Museum für Kommunikation (see page 83), also has interactive displays and is free of charge.

At the Fotografie-Forum International at Weckmarkt 17 there are regular exhibitions by internationally renowned photographers. The gallery shop is a great place to browse if you're searching for original prints and catalogues.

You'll also get the chance to take an extended shopping tour through the boutiques and department stores of the inner city. Head for the Zeilgalerie and the large department stores Karstadt and Galeria Kaufhof, which are all located along Frankfurt's busiest shopping street, the Zeil.

If shopping is not your thing, keep dry and keep sightseeing on board the Ebbelwei Express tram (see page 61). The Nocturnal Animal House and Exotarium at Frankfurter Zoo (see page 61) are sheltered from the elements and will keep children amused.

Or why not treat yourself to the latest cut by one of the city's top hairstylists? The city's many excellent hairstylists are also a good choice if the weather makes you feel like pampering yourself. A couple of tips are expose.deluxe in the Schillerstrasse (see page 68) and Liebesdienste in Sachsenhausen (see page 85). The former is located in an incredibly chic but kid-friendly clothes store with a children's play corner.

Yet another possibility is to get yourself really wet by visiting one of Frankfurt's attractive indoor pools. At Frankfurt's largest indoor swimming complex the Rebstockbad (☎ (069) 708 078 ⓦ www.rebstockbad-frankfurt.de ⓝ S-Bahn: 17; bus: 34, 50 to Rebstockbad) you can enjoy a giant water slide, wave pool and saunas.

🔺 *The hothouses of the Palmengarten are just one option for a wet, cold day*

On arrival

Most travellers on a short visit to Frankfurt will arrive by plane at one of the city's two airports. Frankfurt Rhein-Main Airport is quite close to town, whereas Frankfurt-Hahn is over an hour's drive away. Frankfurt Rhein-Main Airport is linked with the city's public transport network, while there is only a bus connection from Frankfurt-Hahn.

TIME DIFFERENCE
German clocks follow Central European Time (CET). During Daylight Saving Time (end Mar–end Oct), the clocks are put ahead one hour.

ARRIVING
By air
Frankfurt Rhein-Main Airport (Ⓦ www.airportcity-frankfurt.com) is located around 13 km (9 miles) southwest of the city centre. As Europe's second largest airport, it can offer its guests excellent facilities. They include banks, a post office, and numerous restaurants and shops in both terminals, some of which are open 24 hours.

Rail connections to the city centre are excellent. The station for local and regional trains is situated below the airport on Level 1 of Terminal 1. Trains depart regularly for central Frankfurt on a 24-hour basis. Information on tickets and timetables can be obtained at the RMV Mobility Centre at Level 0, Hall B, Terminal 1. Travelling time to downtown Frankfurt is around 15–20 minutes.

Most buses arrive and depart from the stop in front of the arrivals hall at Terminal 1, including bus 61 to Frankfurt SüdBahnhof, in the district of Sachsenhausen. Tickets can be bought from the driver. Many hotels around the airport also provide a free shuttle service. Taxis, the most expensive option, are available outside both terminals. The trip to central Frankfurt will take about 20 minutes in normal traffic and cost at least €30. Those who want to hire a car will find that the major rental car companies are located in both terminals.

Frankfurt-Hahn Situated roughly 125 km (78 miles) southwest of Frankfurt, this airport is the arrival point for low-cost Ryanair flights from Britain. Small in comparison to Rhein-Main Airport, it still offers its guests all the necessary facilities. Major rental car companies at the airport include Avis and Hertz. More information at Ⓦ www.hahn-airport.de. Buses link Frankfurt-Hahn with Frankfurt city and depart from the bus stop in front of the terminal building on the hour between 03.00 and 22.00 with an extra bus at 02.30 and 16.30. The trip to takes 1 hr 45 mins (delays are not uncommon due to heavy motorway traffic) and costs €12. ❶ (06543) 50190 Ⓦ www.bohr-omnibusse.de

By rail

The **Hauptbahnhof** (central railway station) is one of the busiest in Europe; the arrival point for all long-distance trains, it is also a hub of the city's public transport network. The station has excellent facilities, including a tourist office. Most destinations in the city can be reached with S- or U-Bahn trains from here. It is about a 15–20-minute walk to the historic town centre. Long-distance buses from all over Europe also stop in front of the station.

By road

Autobahnen (motorways) converge on Frankfurt from all points of the compass. It is relatively easy to get into the centre (signposted as *Zentrum* or *Stadtmitte*) by just following the motorway signs. There are numerous multi-storey car parks (*Parkhäuser*) in the inner

city – free parking is rare. The one-way-street system and frequent diversions can be confusing.

FINDING YOUR FEET

Because central Frankfurt is quite compact, it doesn't take long to get the hang of the place. There are numerous pedestrian zones in the inner city, so you can stroll around without having to worry too much about traffic. Though there are some seedy sex shops and strip clubs near the main railway station, the inner city is comparatively safe, even at night.

ORIENTATION

From the Hauptbahnhof, Kaiserstrasse leads northeast to the Hauptwache, near the city's main shopping street, the Zeil. Heading south from opposite the Zeilgalerie shopping centre, on the Zeil, Liebfrauenstrasse and Neue Kräme lead to Paulsplatz and the Römerberg, at the heart of Frankfurt's old quarter. Running parallel to the River Main, just south of the Römerberg, is Untermainkai. Two footbridges (Holbeinsteg and Eiserner Steg) cross the river to Schaumainkai (Museumsufer), a street that runs parallel to the river on the Sachsenhausen side of the river.

Navigating around the partly pedestrianised central city area on foot is easy. Landmarks to look for in the centre include the Kaiserdom (Cathedral), the Paulskirche (St Paul's Church) and the skyscrapers of the city area. The River Main is also a good orientation point. Otherwise ask somebody, the chances are high that they'll direct you in English. The maps in this book are up to date and show the main sights and streets in each area, but many of the places that we list are on smaller streets. If you are planning

IF YOU GET LOST, TRY …

Excuse me, do you speak English?
Entschuldigen Sie, sprechen Sie Englisch?
Entshuldigen zee, shprekhen zee english?

Excuse me, is this the right way to the old town/the city centre/the tourist office/ the station/the bus station?
Entschuldigung, geht es hier zur Altstadt/zur Stadtmitte/
zur Touristeninformation/zum Bahnhof/zum BusBahnhof?
*Entshuldeegoong, gayt es here tsoor altshtat/tsoor shtatmitter/
tsoor Touristeninformation/tsoom baanhof/tsoom busbaanhof?*

Can you point to it on my map?
Können Sie es mir bitte auf der Karte zeigen?
Kernen see es meer bitter owf der kaarte tsygen?

to stay in Frankfurt for longer than a couple of days, it's a good idea
to acquire a detailed map, preferably one with a street index, from
a local news-stand or bookshop or from the tourist office.

GETTING AROUND
Frankfurt has a fast and efficient public transport network
comprised of *S-Bahnen* (suburban trains), *U-Bahnen* (underground
trains), *StrassenBahnen* (trams) and buses. Of these, you will find
you can mainly limit yourself to the S-Bahn and U-Bahn lines,
because they will get you to just about anywhere in the city,

Frankfurt

0 ___ 300 metres
0 ___ 300 yards

BOCKENHEIM

Botanischer
Garten

Grüneburgpark

Leipziger Strasse

Bockenheimer
Warte

Senckenberg
Museum

Frankfurt-Hahn

Messe   Messeturm

EUROPA-ALLEE

Galluswarte

Hauptbahnhof

Sommer-
hoffpark

Palmen-
garten

Westend

Festhalle
Messe

Taunusanlage

Main Tower

Oper
Frankfurt

Hauptbahnhof

Westhafen

Main

Holzhausenstr

Alte
Oper

Alte Oper

Jüdisches
Museum

Museum für
Kommunikation

Städel

Grüneburgweg

Börse

Hauptwache

Klein-
markthalle
Goethehaus

Paulskirche

Römer

Museum der
Weltkulturen

Schweizer Platz

Südbahnhof

Frankfurt Rhein-Main

POI
U-Bahn
S-Bahn
Cathedral
Information
Police Station
Airport
Railway Stn
Bus Station
Hospital

52

and environs, that is of interest. If you are just sticking to the inner-city area and Sachsenhausen, it is possible to walk everywhere, as distances aren't great.

Good value, if you want use the public transport network a lot, is the Frankfurt Card. It is valid for one or two days on all public transport in the city and offers reduced entrance fees to many museums and other attractions. It's available from the tourist office. A *Tageskarte* (day ticket) can be bought from one of the ticket machines at S- or U-Bahn stations. With it, you can travel as much as you want on all public transport on that specific day.

The city's *Nachtbuslinien* (night bus lines) are great for late-night revellers. They serve all city districts and depart Konstablerwache every half-hour on Fridays and Saturdays from 01.30 to 03.00. Tickets can be bought from the driver, as is the case with all city buses.

More information, along with maps of the public transport network, is available from the tourist offices and the **Verkehrsinsel** (Mobility Information Centre) at the Hauptwache ❶ (01805) 768 4636 ❾ www.rmv.de ❸ 09.00–20.00 Mon–Fri, 09.30–18.00 Sat

Taxis charge set rates (metered) within the city. During the day, the initial charge is €2, then approximately €1.60 per km for the first 3 km (2 miles). Taxi stands can be found all around the city, or you can hail one from the street. Taxi call centres: **Taxi Zentrale** ❶ (069) 250 001; **Taxirufzentrale** ❶ (069) 230 033

Velo Taxis Beat inner-city taxi jams and take the city's version of oriental bicycle rickshaws. Cheaper than a taxi, and environmentally friendly to boot. ❶ (0700) 8356 8294 ❾ www.0700velotaxi.de

CAR HIRE

Hiring a car is only worthwhile if you want to explore the region surrounding Frankfurt at your own pace – though much can

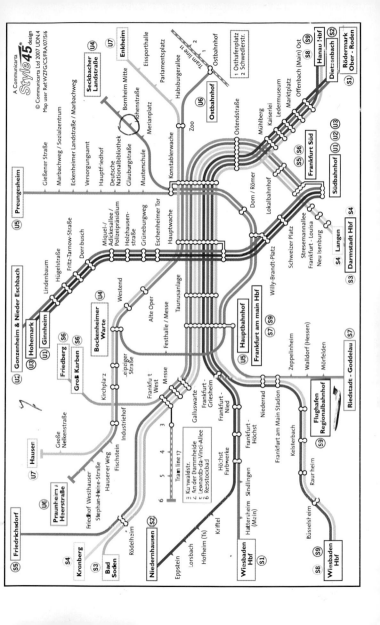

be reached with public transport. For exploring within the city, don't bother. You'll get from A to B quicker with the S- and U-Bahn system.

A small economy class car for one day with unlimited kilometres and compulsory insurance might cost from around €70, a mid-range car for the same period from €85. Rates vary according to season and length of hire, but special offers are available – check the internet. Good deals can also be booked with your airline before you fly.

International rental companies
Avis ❶ (069) 2799 7010 Ⓦ www.avis.de
Budget ❶ (069) 614 004 Ⓦ www.budget.de
Europcar ❶ (069) 242 9810 Ⓦ www.europcar.de
Hertz ❶ (069) 230 484 Ⓦ www.hertz.de
Sixt ❶ (0180) 525 2525 (toll call) Ⓦ www.e-sixt.de

Local rental companies
Alamo ❶ (069) 405 7060 Ⓦ www.alamo.de
Buchbinder rent-a-car ❶ (069) 789 5928
Ⓦ www.buchbinder-rent-a-car.de
Turtle Rent ❶ (069) 610 9490 Ⓦ www.turtlerent.de

❶ *Skyscrapers and 19th-century mansions often sit side by side in Frankfurt*

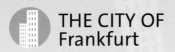

The Centre & Nordend

If you are new to Frankfurt, explore this part of town first. Within a relatively compact area, you will find many of the city's main sights and attractions, such as the rebuilt Römerberg, which marks the historic core of 'Old Frankfurt', or the Zeil, one of Germany's busiest shopping streets. Further north, away from the hectic pace of the inner city, is the Main Cemetery, which is also one of Frankfurt's most beautiful parks.

In this part of town you will find dozens of restaurants and cafés, nightclubs, discos, bars and parks where you can picnic. In the Alte Oper (Old Opera House) you can enjoy concerts ranging from classical to pop. In summer the inner-city streets come alive with festivals and street performances, while in winter the Römerberg makes the perfect setting for a fairytale Christmas market. The area is small enough to walk around, though the Hauptwache and Konstablerwache U- and S-Bahn stations can spare you sore feet.

SIGHTS & ATTRACTIONS

Alte Oper (Old Opera House)

The splendid neoclassical style Old Opera House is a 1981 reconstruction of the building destroyed in 1944. For a long time it was regarded as the loveliest ruin in what was formerly West Germany. A new opera house was built in 1951 so the Alte Oper is now used as a concert hall.
ⓐ Opernpl. 1 ① Ticket hotline (069) 134 0400 ⓦ www.alteoper.de
Ⓝ U-Bahn: 6, 7 to Alte Oper

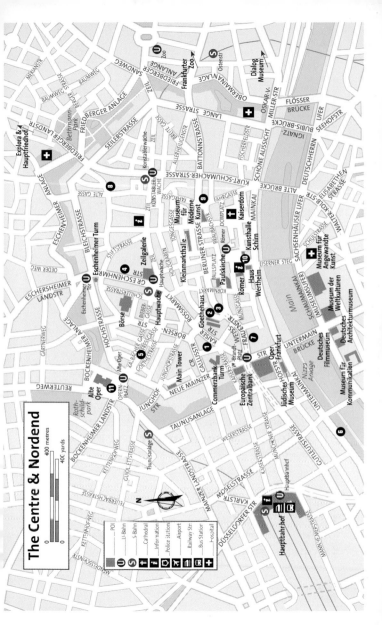

The Centre & Nordend

0 ————— 400 meters
0 ————— 400 yards

Legend:
- POI
- U-Bahn
- S-Bahn
- Cathedral
- Information
- Police station
- Airport
- Railway Stn
- Bus Station
- Hospital

Labels on map:

Zoo
Frankfurter Zoo
Dialog Museum
FLÖSSER BRÜCKE
Explora & Hauptfriedhof
Rothschild-park
Alte Oper
Alte Oper 11
Börse
Hauptwache
Eschenheimer Turm
Zeil
Zeil
Konstablerwache
KONSTABLER WACHE
Zellgalerie
Kleinmarkthalle
Museum für Moderne Kunst
Kaiserdom
Kunsthalle Schirn
Paulskirche
Römer
Haus Wertheim
Goethehaus
Main Tower
Commerzbank Turm
Europäische Zentralbank
Oper Frankfurt
Jüdisches Museum
Deutsches Filmmuseum
Deutsches Architekturmuseum
Museum der Weltkulturen
Museum für Angewandte Kunst
Museum für Kommunikation
Main
EISERNER STEG
UNTERMAINBRÜCKE
ALTE BRÜCKE
Hauptbahnhof

Numbered POIs: 1, 2, 3, 4, 5, 6, 7, 8, 9, 10, 11

AN INNER-CITY WALK

Leave the railway station and walk along Kaiserstrasse, passing the European Central Bank and Frankfurt's noblest hotel, the Frankfurter Hof. It will take about 15 mins to reach the baroque Hauptwache. For shopping turn right onto the pedestrianised Zeil. Otherwise, go left into Biebergasse. Branching right, Schillerstrasse will bring you to Börsenplatz, the site of the Stock Exchange. Return to Biebergasse, cross Börsenstrasse and follow the pedestrianised Kalbächer Gasse towards the Alte Oper. In summer, outdoor concerts take place on the square in front. Return to Börsenstrasse via Grosser Bockenheimer Strasse, also known as Fressgasse (Feeding Lane) because of its many restaurants and delis. Via Steinweg you will soon arrive back at the Hauptwache and Zeil. From the Zeilgalerie head south along Liebfrauenstrasse and Neue Kräme to Paulsplatz, the site of the Paulskirche. Now it's only a stone's throw to the museums and picturesque buildings on the Römerberg. The cathedral is reached from Römerplatz via a narrow street that runs between the Kunstverein and Schirn Kunsthalle. Leave the Römerberg and follow Limpurger Gasse and Münzgasse to Willy-Brandt-Platz. Turn right to reach Kaiserstrasse, which quickly brings you back to the railway station.

Börse (Stock Exchange)

Housed in an imposing 19th-century structure, the Stock Exchange is fronted by a sculpture depicting a bull and a bear. The former symbolises rising prices, the latter falling prices. Though

administration and computerised trading is now handled by the
Neue Börse, classic floor trading still takes place here. ❸ Börsenpl. 2–4
❶ (069) 2111 1515 Ⓦ www.deutsche-boerse.com ⓛ Free guided tours
in English 10.00, 11.00, 12.00 Mon–Fri. Book 24 hours in advance,
photo ID needed ⓝ U-Bahn & S-Bahn to Hauptwache

Ebbelwei-Express (Apple Wine Express)

The historic Ebbelwei-Express tram tours the city's main attractions
on Saturday and Sunday afternoons. These one-hour trips start and
end at the zoo, though you can get on and off at any of the stops,
such as the Hauptbahnhof. Apple wine and apple juice are included
in the price. Buy your ticket from the driver. ❶ (069) 2132 2425
Ⓦ www.ebbelwei-express.com ⓛ 13.30–17.35 Sat & Sun

Eschenheimer Turm

There were once around 60 towers ringing the city, but this medieval
defensive tower is the most impressive of the few that remain.
There is a popular restaurant at its base. ❸ Eschenheimer Tor
ⓝ U-Bahn: 1–3 to Eschenheimer Tor

Frankfurter Zoo

One of the oldest zoos in the world, including a free-flight aviary
and a nocturnal house. Children will love the Exotarium, with its
crocodiles, giant snakes and cute penguins. ❸ Alfred-Brehm-Pl. 16
❶ (069) 2123 3735 Ⓦ www.zoo-frankfurt.de ⓛ 09.00–19.00 (summer);
09.00–17.00 (winter) ⓝ U-Bahn: 6, 7 to Zoo

Hauptfriedhof (Main cemetery)

Regarded as one of the loveliest of Frankfurt's many parks, the
cemetery was landscaped in the English style in the early 19th

century. Among the distinguished locals buried here is the philosopher Arthur Schopenhauer. Next door is the Alter Jüdischer Friedhof (Old Jewish Cemetery), where members of the wealthy Rothschild banking dynasty are buried. ⓐ Eckenheimer Landstr. 194 ⓦ www.frankfurter-hauptfriedhof.de ⓝ U-Bahn: 5 to Hauptfriedhof

Haus Wertheim

Take a look at the outside of the sole remaining Tudor-style house in Frankfurt's Old Town to have survived World War II bombing. Built around 1600, the house is a typical merchant's house for the period. ⓐ Fahrtor 1 ⓝ U-Bahn: 4, 5 to Römer

Kaiserdom (Imperial Cathedral)

The Gothic Imperial Cathedral was the place where, for many centuries, German emperors were elected and crowned. The term *Dom*, (cathedral), is a misnomer because Frankfurt was never the seat of a bishop. There are great views from the 96 m (315 ft) tower (see page 66 for Museum). ⓐ Dompl. 14 ⓦ www.dom-frankfurt.de ⓝ U-Bahn: 4, 5 to Dom or Römer

Nizza Anlage (Nissa Garden)

Fig, orange and palm trees are normally exotic species in Germany, but these beautiful gardens on the Main lie in the one of the warmest spots in Frankfurt and there are more than 150 plant species growing there. Planted in 1875, the Mediterranean park has numerous benches and is close to Nizza am Main (see page 71). ⓐ Untermainkai ⓝ U-Bahn: 1–5 to Willy-Brandt-Pl.

⦿ *The bull and bear in front of the Börse symbolise rising and falling prices*

Paulskirche (St Paul's Church)

Shaped as an ellipse with a tower in front, St Paul's Church was built between 1789 and 1833. In 1944 the church was completely gutted, but was rebuilt with donations that poured in from all over Germany. The German National Assembly met here in 1848, as part of one of the earliest attempts to set up a democratic constitution in this country. A commemorative plaque is dedicated to John F Kennedy, who spoke in front of the church in June 1963. ❸ Paulspl. 🕙 10.00–17.00 🚇 U-Bahn: 4, 5 to Dom or Römer; tram: 11 to Römer

Römerberg

A tourist magnet, the Römerberg was once the centre of Germany's largest medieval *Altstadt*, or historic town quarter. After devastating bombing in 1944 there was virtually nothing left of the more than 2,000 buildings that once existed here. The picturesque edifices now lining the *Römerplatz* (square) are all reconstructions. You can visit the Römer complex, Frankfurt's former town hall, with its portraits of Germany's 52 Holy Roman Emperors in the *Kaisersaal* (Imperial banquet hall). Though the Römer was rebuilt in the 1950s, the half-timbered buildings opposite weren't reconstructed until 1986. The square also contains the Gothic church **Alte Nikolaikirche** (Old St Nicholas) and several cafés and restaurants. There are numerous events during summer. ❸ Kaisersaal in Römer 🕙 10.00–13.00, 14.00–17.00 🚇 U-Bahn: 4, 5 to Dom or Römer

Streets & streetlife

On weekdays the Zeil is always lively, and in the warmer months there are numerous street performers. Goethestrasse is good for browsing through exclusive boutiques, while Schillerstrasse has an interesting food market on Fridays. The place to go for tasty, if pricey, snacks is Fressgasse. The outdoor cafés are great for people-watching.

Views

The 200m-high Main Tower (see page 13) gives great views but there is an admission charge. The Kaiserdom (cathedral) tower offers great views towards the Römerberg, while the views from the top of Zeilgalerie shopping centre (on the Zeil) are not only great, but also free.

CULTURE

Dialog Museum

Discover what it is like to live in darkness in this extraordinary museum. Blind tour guides will take you through the exhibition made up of sounds, smells and textures. Bookings necessary.
ⓐ Hanauer Landstr. 145, Ostend ❶ Bookings 0700 4455 6000
ⓦ www.dialogmuseum.de ❶ 09.00–17.00 Tues–Fri, 11.00–19.00 Sat & Sun. Open first Thur in the month until 21.00. ⓝ U-Bahn: 6 to Ostbahnhof

Explora

This hands-on science museum, with its interactive exhibits, is a fun place for both kids and adults. Check out the 'Rock 'n' Roll' machine.
ⓐ Glauburgpl. 1 ❶ (069) 788 888 ⓦ www.exploramuseum.de
❶ 11.00–18.00 Tues–Sun ⓝ U-Bahn: 5 to Glauburgstr.

Goethehaus & Museum

The house where Goethe, Germany's greatest literary genius, was born in 1749, is a faithful reconstruction of the building destroyed in

World War II. Its interior is decorated according to the fashion of the time, and includes an original desk at which Goethe worked on such classics as *The Sorrows of Young Werther*. The museum displays his hand-written texts and portraits by contemporaries. Guided tours are only available in German, but there are audio-visual guides for hire in English. ⓐ Grosser Hirschgraben 23–24 ① (069) 138 800 ⓦ www.goethehaus-frankfurt.de ① 10.00–18.00 Mon–Sat, 10.00–17.00 Sun ⓝ U Bahn: 1 5 to Willy-Brandt-Pl.

Jüdisches Museum (Jewish Museum)

An insight into the life of Frankfurt's Jewish population, from the 12th century until the Holocaust. ⓐ Untermainkai 14–15 ① (069) 2123 5000 ⓦ www.juedischesmuseum.de ① 10.00–17.00 Thur–Sun & Tues, 10.00–20.00 Wed ⓝ U-Bahn: 1–5 to Willy-Brandt-Pl. Admission free last Sat in the month

Kaiserdom & Museum

The cathedral interior boasts a number of significant works of art, including a life-size calvary scene in stone (1509). The museum displays a silver bust of the unfortunate St Bartholomew who, according to legend, was skinned alive. ⓐ Dompl. 14 ① (069) 1337 6186 ⓦ www.dom-frankfurt.de ① 10.00–17.00 Tues–Fri, 11.00–17.00 Sat & Sun; Guided tours 15.00 ⓝ U-Bahn: 4, 5 to Römer

Kunsthalle Schirn (Schirn Art Gallery)

Well-known modern art institution featuring regular exhibitions. ⓐ Römerberg 6 (069) 299 8820 ⓦ www.schirn.de ① 10.00–19.00 Fri–Sun & Tues, 10.00–22.00 Wed & Thur ⓝ U-Bahn: 4, 5 to Römer; tram 11, 12 to Paulskirche

Museum für Moderne Kunst (Modern Art Museum)

Referred to as the *Tortenstück* (slice of cake) due to its unusual triangular shape, this building houses 60s and 70s art from the likes of Andy Warhol, Roy Lichtenstein, Jasper Johns and Joseph Beuys. Part of the collection also focuses on more contemporary art. Free guided tours available, see the website for dates and times. ⓐ Domstr. 10 ☎ (069) 2123 0447 Ⓦ www.mmk-frankfurt.de ⏰ 10.00–17.00 Thur–Sun & Tues, 10.00–20.00 Wed Ⓝ U-Bahn: 4, 5 to Römer

RETAIL THERAPY

SHOPPING STREETS & MARKETS

Frankfurt's main shopping streets are the Zeil (pedestrianised, huge range of top stores), Goethestrasse (exclusive, upmarket shopping), Schillerstrasse (pedestrianised, quality shops, good range of restaurants), Grosse Bockenheimer Strasse, otherwise known as Fressgasse (between Opernplatz and Börsenstrasse, has restaurants, cafés, fancy boutiques, delicatessens) and Berger Strasse (colourful mix of boutiques, organic food shops, discounters and traditional *Ebbelwei* taverns). Lively food markets are found at Konstablerwache (⏰ 10.00–20.00 Thur, 08.00–17.00 Sat), and Schillerstrasse (⏰ 09.00–18.30 Fri).

Azita Funky skateboard label selling clothes and accessories, plus limited edition products designed by showcased artists. ⓐ Munzgasse 10 ☎ (069) 2197 9644 Ⓦ www.azitastore.com ⏰ 11.00–20.00 Mon–Fri, 10.00–19.00 Sat Ⓝ U-Bahn:1–5 to Willy-Brandt-Pl.

Bitter & Zart A wonderful range of fine chocolate.
ⓐ Domstr. 4 ⓣ (069) 9494 2846 ⓦ www.bitterundzart.de
ⓛ 10.00–19.00 Mon–Fri, 10.00–16.00 Sat ⓝ U-Bahn: 4, 5 to Römer

The British Bookshop English-language literature.
ⓐ Börsenstr. 17 ⓣ (069) 280 492 ⓦ www.british-bookshop.de
ⓛ 09.30–19.00 Mon–Fri, 09.30–18.00 Sat ⓝ U-Bahn: 1–3, 6, 7;
S-Bahn: 1–6, 8, 9 to Hauptwache

Delirium Voted several times as Germany's best music store,
Delirium focuses on electronica, techno and house, plus club
fashion. ⓐ Töngesgasse 38 ⓣ (069) 1310 169 ⓦ www.delirium.de
ⓛ 11.00–20.00 Mon–Fri, 11.00–19.00 Sat ⓝ U-Bahn: 4–7;
S-Bahn: 1–6, 8, 9 to Konstablerwache

expose.deluxe Stylish store selling internationally recognised
designer labels at low prices. A chic stop for an espresso. Has a
children's play corner, great take-away sushi and a hairdresser.
ⓐ Schillerstr. 27–29 ⓣ (069) 9288 2621, Hairdresser (069) 9288 2623
ⓦ www.exposedeluxe.com ⓛ 11.00–20.00 Mon–Fri, 10.00–18.00 Sat
ⓝ U-Bahn: 1–3, 6, 7; S-Bahn: 1–6, 8 to Hauptwache

Galeria Kaufhof Large department store, good for clothing,
electrical goods and music. The food section is a good place
to stock up for picnics. ⓐ Zeil 116–126 ⓣ (069) 219 10
ⓦ www.galeria-kaufhof.de ⓛ 09.30–20.00 Mon–Wed,
09.30–21.00 Thur–Sat ⓝ U-Bahn: Hauptwache

◗ *The Fressgasse is a popular spot for lunch and shopping*

Hugendubel Great range of German-language books. Also a good map section. ⓐ Steinweg 12 ⓣ (01801) 484 484 ⓦ www.hugendubel.de ⓛ 09.30–20.00 Mon–Wed, 09.30–21.00 Thur–Sat ⓝ U-Bahn: 1–3, 6, 7; S-Bahn: 1–6, 8, 9 to Hauptwache

Kleinmarkthalle This covered food market is fun to explore. Try the Markt-Stubb restaurant upstairs. ⓐ Hasengasse 5–7 ⓛ 07.30–18.00 Mon–Fri, 07.30–15.00 Sat ⓝ U-Bahn: 4–7; S-Bahn: 1–6, 8, 9 to Konstablerwache

Parfümerie Douglas A huge range of cosmetics, perfumes and beauty care articles for both girls and guys. ⓐ Zeil 100 ⓣ (069) 1338 69150 ⓦ www.douglas.de ⓛ 10.00–20.00 Mon–Sat ⓝ U-Bahn: Hauptwache

Zeilgalerie More than 50 shops, restaurants and eateries over seven floors. Great views from the restaurant at the top. ⓐ Zeil 112–114 ⓦ www.zeilgalerie.de ⓛ Store 10.00–20.00 Mon–Sat ⓝ U-Bahn: 1, 2, 3, 6, 7 to Hauptwache

TAKING A BREAK

Altes Café Schneider £ ❶ A charmingly old-fashioned café, serving scrumptious cakes. Their gift-wrapped boxes of Bethmännchen (traditional marzipan biscuits) make a nice gift. ⓐ Kaiserstr. 12 ⓣ (069) 281 447 12 ⓛ 08.00–19.00 Mon–Fri, 08.00–18.00 Sat, 12.00–18.00 Sun ⓝ U-Bahn: 1–3, 6, 7; S-Bahn: 1, 6, 8, 9 to Hauptwache

Café Karin £ ❷ Relaxed mix of café, bar and restaurant, with a younger crowd. Lunches are reasonably priced. ⓐ Grosser Hirschgraben 28 ⓣ (069) 295217 ⓛ 09.00–01.00 Mon–Sat, 10.00–01.00 Sun ⓝ U-Bahn: 1–3, 6, 7; S-Bahn: 1–6, 8, 9 to Hauptwache

Café Riz £ ❸ A 1950s style café that attracts the alternative scene. Comfy sofas and deer horns on the walls. Great salad bar, crêpes and snacks. ⓐ Berliner Str. 72 ⓣ (069) 282 439 ⓛ 10.00–01.00 Mon–Thur & Sun, 10.00–03.00 Fri & Sat ⓝ U-Bahn: 1–3, 6, 7 to Hauptwache

Eissalon Fontanella £ ❹ Freshly made Italian ice cream and strong espresso. ⓐ Grosse Eschenheimer Str. 16–18 ⓣ (069) 2424 7072 ⓛ 09.00–22.30 Mon–Sat, 10.00–22.30 Sun ⓝ U-Bahn: 1–3 to Eschenheimer Tor

Ima Multibar £ ❺ This tiny bar serves tasty smoothies and wraps and crunchy fresh salads. Artworks and photos decorate the walls, and there are DJs some evenings. ⓐ Kleine Bockenheimer Str. 14 ⓣ (069) 9002 5665 ⓛ 11.00–21.30 Mon–Wed, 11.00–01.30 Thur–Sat (kitchen closes 24.00) ⓝ U-Bahn: 1–3, 6, 7; S-Bahn: 1, 6, 8, 9 to Hauptwache

Nizza am Main £ ❻ With a great location in the Nizza Gardens, this upmarket restaurant offers an affordable lunch until 15.00. ⓐ Untermainkai 17 ⓣ (069) 2992 07511 ⓦ www.nizzamain.de ⓛ 11.00–late Mon–Fri, 12.00–late Sat & Sun ⓝ U-Bahn/S-Bahn: Frankfurt Hbf

AFTER DARK

RESTAURANTS

Klosterhof £ ❼ Hearty portions of meat and good beer.
A popular lunch spot too. ⓐ Weissfrauenstr. 3 ❶ (069) 9139 9000
ⓦ www.klosterhof-frankfurt.de ⓛ 11.30 –01.00 Mon–Fri, 17.00–01.00
Sat & Sun (kitchen closes 23.30) ⓝ U-Bahn: 1–5; tram: 11, 12 to
Willy-Brandt-Pl.

Rama V ££ ❽ Delicious Thai food and good cocktails. Reservations
recommended. ⓐ Vilbeler Str. 32 ❶ (069) 2199 6488 ⓛ 12.00–14.30,
18.00–24.00 Mon–Sat (kitchen closes 23.30). ⓝ U-Bahn: 4–7; S-Bahn:
1–6, 8, 9 to Konstablerwache

Sardegna ££ ❾ Friendly restaurant with traditional Sardinian fare.
Reservations recommended. ⓐ Fahrgasse 84 ❶ (069) 1337 6779
ⓦ www.ristorante-sardegna-ffm.de ⓛ 11.30–01.00 (kitchen closes
23.30) ⓝ U-Bahn: 4–7; S-Bahn: 1–6, 8 to Konstablerwache

Zum Schwarzen Stern ££ ❿ Good German style food, great location
on the picturesque Römerberg. Reservations recommended.
ⓐ Römerberg 6 ❶ (069) 291 979 ⓦ www.schwarzerstern.de
ⓛ 11.30–23.00 (summer unless raining, in which case use winter
times); 11.30–14.30, 18.00–22.00 (winter) ⓝ U-Bahn: 4, 5 to Römer

Opéra £££ ⓫ The historic foyer of the Alte Oper provides
a magnificent setting for an evening meal. Outdoor dining on
the terrace in summer. Reservations recommended. ⓐ Opernpl. 1
❶ (069) 134 0215 ⓛ 12.00–01.00 (kitchen closes 23.00) ⓝ U-Bahn:
6, 7 to Alte Oper

BARS, CLUBS & DISCOS

Jazzkeller One of Germany's most famous jazz clubs. Jam
session every Wednesday, Latin-Funk dance night every Friday.
🅐 Kleine Bockenheimer Str. 18a 🕽 (069) 288 537 🅦 www.jazzkeller.de
🅝 U-Bahn: 4–7; S-Bahn: 1–6, 8, 9 to Konstablerwache

Latin Palace Chango Giant Latin disco with two dance floors
opposite the central station. Dance the night away to salsa,
merengue, reggaeton and more. 🅐 Münchnerstr. 57 🕽 (069) 2722 0807
🅦 www.latinpalace-chango.de 🕒 20.00–late Thur–Sat 🅝 U-Bahn:
1–9 to Hauptbahnhof

Living XXL Upmarket dining and dance venue. Friday evenings for
1980s classics, Saturdays for house and soul music. 🅐 Kaiserstr. 29
🅦 www.livingxxl.de 🕒 Dining from 18.30 Wed–Sun, Disco from
22.00 Thur–Sat 🅝 U-Bahn: 1–5 to Willy-Brandt-Pl. Admission charge

Studio Bar Good music, an extensive range of cocktails and
whisky, and a trendy interior make this bar a popular place.
🅐 Katharinenpforte 6 🕒 18.00–01.00 Mon–Thur, 18.00–02.00 Fri,
20.00–02.00 Sat 🅝 U-Bahn: 1–3, 6, 7; S-Bahn: 1–6, 8, 9 to Hauptwache

Unity 1 Club with a Middle Eastern atmosphere and rotating DJs,
playing music from Indian vibes to reggae and soul. In summer,
chill out in the giant Bedouin tent covering the courtyard and
drink mint tea. 🅐 Hanauer Landstr. 2 🕽 (069) 9434 0555
🅦 www.unity1.de 🕒 20.00 late Tues– Sun 🅝 S-Bahn: 1–6, 8, 9
to Ostendstr.

CINEMAS & THEATRES

Alte Oper The main address for major classical, jazz and pop concerts.
🅐 Opernpl. 1 🚹 Tickets (069) 134 0400 🚆 www.alteoper.de
🚇 U-Bahn: 6, 7 to Alte Oper

Oper Frankfurt The city's opera is first rate, with a repertoire
that includes both classical and modern performances.
🅐 Untermainanlage 11 🚹 Tickets (069) 134 0400
🚆 www.oper-frankfurt.de 🚇 U-Bahn: 1–5 to Willy-Brandt-Pl.

Schauspiel Avant-garde works as well as traditional theatre.
Bucovinaclub in the foyer. 🅐 Neue Mainzer Str. 17 🚹 Tickets
(069) 134 0400 🚆 www.schauspielfrankfurt.de 🚇 U-Bahn: 1–5
to Willy-Brandt-Pl.

Turm-Palast Current Hollywood films in English. 🅐 Bleichstr. 57
🚹 (069) 281 787 🚇 U-Bahn: 1–3 to Eschenheimer Tor

NIGHT-TIME VIEWS

The views over Frankfurt's skyline from the top of the Zeilgalerie,
or the Dinea restaurant in the **Galeria Kaufhof** building, can be
stunning at night 🚇 U-Bahn: 1, 2, 3, 6, 7 to Hauptwache

◀ *Frankfurt's historic Alte Oper*

Sachsenhausen

Sachsenhausen, on the south side of the river, is famed for the *Ebbelwei* (apple wine) taverns of picturesque *Altsachsenhausen* (Old Sachsenhausen), and the excellent museums that line Schaumainkai. The district did not suffer as badly as the rest of Frankfurt during World War II, so you can get a better impression of what the medieval city looked like. Schweizer Strasse is the main shopping street and is lined with *Ebbelwei* taverns, exclusive boutiques, cafés and gourmet shops.

Sachsenhausen is easy to explore on foot, and is especially nice along the banks of the River Main and through the cobbled streets of Old Sachsenhausen. The U-Bahn station Schweizer Platz and the S-Bahn stations Lokalbahnhof and Frankfurt Süd provide quick access to points further away. The pedestrian bridges Holbeinsteg and Eiserner Steg link Sachsenhausen with the inner city.

SIGHTS & ATTRACTIONS

Altsachsenhausen

Over-commercialised and somewhat seedy in places, the cobbled streets and half-timbered houses of Old Sachsenhausen still possess a certain charm. Check out Schellgasse 8 (northwest of Elisabethenstrasse, off Dreikönigsstrasse), the city's oldest half-timbered building, built in1291. Nestled between Elisabethenstrasse and Dreieichstrasse, the atmosphere in Altsachsenhausen has a small town feel and at night the district comes alive with bars, pubs and typical *Ebbelwei* taverns.

Apfelweinlokale (Apple wine pubs)

The traditional apple wine taverns of Sachsenhausen are popular with locals and tourists alike. Guests usually sit at long rustic

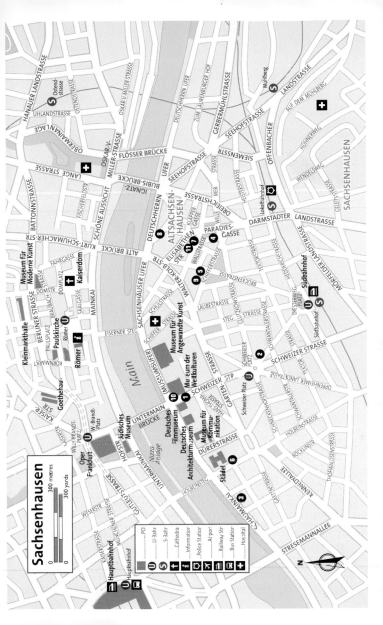

EBBELWEI

Apple wine, variously called *Ebbelwoi, Stöffche, Rauscher, Äppelwoi, Äppelwei*, has been Frankfurt's so-called national drink from the 16th century. According to one legend it was the corpulent Emperor Karl who discovered the drink when he accidentally sat on an apple and squeezed out all the juice. Beware its stomach cleansing qualities, as the drink is renowned for making those unaccustomed to it rush for the loo.

wooden tables to drink sour-tasting apple wine served from a glazed pottery jug known as a *Bembel*. Food is hearty and generally meat, though salads are becoming more popular. The best places to look for *Apfelweinlokale* (also called *Ebbelwoilokale*) are Altsachsenhausen and along Schweizer Strasse (U-Bahn: 1–3 to Schweizer Pl.)

Boating on the River Main

River cruises leave from the Mainkai (north) bank of the river, near the Eiserner Steg. Trips include day cruises on the Rhine to Rüdesheim and Bingen, 50-minute sightseeing cruises, dinner cruises, 'after work' party sailings with DJs on board and special cruises to watch fireworks displays during summer. If you want to paddle yourself, then cross the Eiserner Steg to the opposite bank and hire one of the pedalos.

Primus-Linie (boat cruises) Kiosk Mainkai, Eiserner Steg
 07.45–19.15 Apr–mid-Oct. Ticket office Haus Mainkai 36

 Watching a live match at one of Sachsenhausen's pubs

① (069) 133 8370 **Ⓦ** www.primus-linie.de **Ⓛ** 08.00–16.30 Mon–Fri
Bootshaus Wotan (pedalos) **Ⓐ** Eiserner Steg, Sachsenhäuser Ufer
① (069) 617 566 **Ⓛ** 10.00–23.00 depending on weather

Flohmarkt (Flea market)

Saturday mornings on the Sachsenhäuser embankment, offering everything from genuine antiques to genuine rubbish. Get there early and haggle for the bargains. **Ⓐ** Schaumainkai **Ⓛ** 08.00–14.00 **Ⓝ** U-Bahn: 1–3 to Schweizer Pl.

◉ *Relax with a river cruise down the Main*

Mainufer (River embankments)

The riverside parks are great for strolling, picnicking, sitting in the shade and watching the people and boats go cruising by. Particularly attractive on the north (Römerberg) bank is the so-called Nizza Anlage (see page 62).

Museumsufer (Museum Embankment)

Seven museums lining the Schaumainkai, a couple of international importance. Don't miss the annual Museumsuferfest in August.

⊘ U-Bahn: 1–3 to Schweizer Pl.

Views

Good views of the city skyline from anywhere along Schaumainkai, but the slightly more elevated positions of the two pedestrian bridges Eiserner Steg and Holbeinsteg are even better.

CULTURE

Deutsches Architekturmuseum

The museum building was designed by Oswald Mathias Ungers, and his eye-opening *House in House* is a feature of the museum. Large-scale models, exhibitions and sketches offer a fascinating insight into mankind's progress from primitive dwellings to the high-rise cities of the modern age. ⓐ Schaumainkai 43 ⓘ (069) 2123 8844 ⓦ www.dam-online.de ⓒ 11.00–18.00 Tues–Sun, 12.00–20.00 Wed ⓝ U-Bahn: 1–3 to Schweizer Pl.

Deutsches Filmmuseum

A must for movie fans, the German Film Museum explains the origins and history of modern cinema. You can watch classics from the age of silent movies to the advent of the talkies. ⓐ Schaumainkai 41 ⓘ (069) 9612 20220 ⓦ www.deutschesfilmmuseum.de ⓒ 10.00–17.00 Tues, Thur & Fri, 10.00–19.00 Wed & Sun, 14.00–19.00 Sat ⓝ U-Bahn: 1–3 to Schweizer Pl.

Museum für Angewandte Kunst (Museum of Applied Art)

Designed by American star architect Richard Meier, the Museum of Applied Art is one of the most important museums of its kind. Its collections display arts and crafts from various cultures

spanning 6,000 years. 🄰 Schaumainkai 17 ☎ (069) 2123 4037
🅆 www.museumfuerangewandtekunst.frankfurt.de 🕒 10.00–17.00
Thurs–Sun & Tues, 10.00–21.00 Wed 🄽 U-Bahn: 1–3 to Schweizer Pl.

Museum für Kommunikation

Ever wonder what you would do without your mobile phone?
This interactive museum focuses on all forms of communication,
from beating drums to surfing the web. 🄰 Schaumainkai 53
☎ (069) 60 600 🅆 www.museumsstiftung.de 🕒 09.00–18.00
Tues–Fri, 11.00–19.00 Sat & Sun 🄽 U-Bahn: 1–3 to Schweizer Pl.

Museum der Weltkulturen

This anthropology museum, one of the most important in
Germany, holds continually changing exhibitions on topics from
piercings to musical influences. The gallery shows contemporary
art from Africa, Asia, India and Oceania. 🄰 Schaumainkai 29–37
☎ (069) 2123 5913 🅆 www.mdw.frankfurt.de 🕒 10.00–17.00
Thur–Sun &Tues, 10.00–20.00 Wed 🄽 U-Bahn: 1–3 to Schweizer Pl.

Städelsches Kunstinstitut (Städel) (City Art Institute)

One of Germany's most important art museums, the Städel
is a treasure trove of masterpieces from seven centuries.
Collections include Botticelli, Jan van Eyck, Dürer and Holbein, as
well as Renoir, Manet, Matisse and Picasso. Holbein's is a good café.
🄰 Schaumainkai 63 ☎ (069) 605 0980 🅆 www.staedelmuseum.de
🕒 10.00–18.00 Fri–Sun & Tues, 10.00–21.00 Wed & Thur
🄽 U-Bahn: 1–3 to Schweizer Pl.

RETAIL THERAPY

Sachsenhausen's main shopping street is Schweizer Strasse, with its exclusive boutiques, lifestyle shops, cafés, bars, restaurants, delicatessens and apple wine taverns. Don't miss the annual Schweizer Strassenfest in mid-July, with its live music, fashion show and food stalls. Ⓝ U-Bahn: 1–3 to Schweizer Pl.

Äpplergalerie In the café you can sample *Ebbelwei* and other local specialities, while the gift-shop sells typical Frankfurt souvenirs such as *Bembel* – pottery jugs for serving *Ebbelwei*. Ⓐ Klappergasse 9 ❶ (069) 6199 5393 Ⓦ www.aepplergalerie.com Ⓛ 10.30–20.00 Mon–Thur, 10.00–01.00 Fri, 16.00–01.00 Sat Ⓝ S-Bahn: 2, 5, 6 to Lokalbahnhof

Confiserie Chocolaterie Georg Jamin Souvenir chocolates and traditional *Bethmännchen* cookies. Ⓐ Schweizer Str. 54a ❶ (069) 615 619 Ⓦ www.jamin-frankfurt.de Ⓛ 10.00–18.00 Mon–Fri, 09.30–15.00 Sat Ⓝ U-Bahn: 1–3 to Schweizer Pl.

Drauf & Dran Clothing, tattoos and piercings, with women's fashion by young local designers. Ⓐ Brückenstr. 54 ❶ (069) 6637 4790 Ⓦ www.drauf-und-dran.de Ⓛ 13.00–20.00 Mon, Tues, Thur & Fri, 11.00–15.00 Sat Ⓝ U-Bahn: 1–3 to Schweizer Pl.

Ich war ein Dirndl Kitsch hand-made clothing and home accessories sewn from old materials. Ⓐ Brückenstr. 52 ❶ (069) 6612 7744 Ⓦ www.ichwareindirndl.de Ⓛ 11.00–20.00 Mon–Fri, 11.00–16.00 Sat Ⓝ Tram: 14 to Frankensteiner Pl.

Liebesdienste Trendy hairstyles, professional make-up, and the latest fashion accessories at this exclusive beauty studio. ⓐ Textorstr. 24 ⓣ (069) 6062 9760 ⓦ www.liebesdienste-am-main.de ⓛ 09.00–20.00 Mon–Sat ⓝ U-Bahn: 1–3; S-Bahn: 2–6 to Frankfurt Süd

Meyer Feinkost Along with sausages, salamis, cheese, and salads, this deli sells wine, olive oils and locally baked organic bread. Great take-away desserts. ⓐ Schweizer Str. 42 ⓣ (069) 615 010 ⓦ www.meyer-frankfurt.de ⓛ 07.30–19.00 Mon–Fri, 07.30–15.00 Sat ⓝ U-Bahn: 1–3 to Schweizer Pl.

No. 2 One of the best places in Frankfurt for second-hand records. ⓐ Wallstr. 15 ⓣ (069) 624 121 ⓛ 11.00–18.30 Tues–Fri, 10.00–14.00 Sat ⓝ U-Bahn: 1–3 to Schweizer Pl.; bus: 30, 36 to Elisabethenstr

Secondelle Exclusive second-hand clothing, including Chanel and Dolce & Gabbana. ⓐ Schweizer Str. 98 ⓣ (069) 627 776 ⓛ 10.00–19.00 Mon–Fri, 10.00–14.00 Sat ⓝ U-Bahn: 1–3 to Schweizer Pl.

Shoes & News Quality shoes, bags and accessories at moderate prices. ⓐ Mörfelder Landstr. 109a ⓣ (069) 972 6560 ⓛ 09.30–18 30 Mon–Fri, 09.30–16.00 Sat ⓝ U-Bahn: 1–3; S-Bahn: 3–6 to Frankfurt Süd

TeeDeUm Located in an old villa, this stylish speciality food shop sells fine teas, coffee, oil, vinegar and herbs. ⓐ Schweizer Str. 54a ⓣ (069) 9624 8955 ⓛ 10.00–18.30 Mon–Fri, 10.00–16.00 Sat ⓝ U-Bahn: 1 3 to Schweizer Pl.

TAKING A BREAK

Café Bar £ ❶ The breakfast buffet on Sundays is excellent value. Stylish surroundings. 🅐 Schweizer Str. 14 ☎ (069) 622 393 🅦 www.cafebar-frankfurt.de 🕓 12.00–01.00 Mon–Thur, 12.00–02.00 Fri, 11.00–02.00 Sat, 11.00–18.00 Sun 🅝 U-Bahn: 1–3 to Schweizer Pl.

Café Fellini £ ❷ Italian flair on the Schweizer Platz. 🅐 Diesterwegstr. 1 ☎ (069) 9623 0817 🕓 07.30–22.00 Mon–Fri, 0800–1900 Sat 🅝 U-Bahn: 1–3 to Schweizer Pl.

Café im Liebieghaus £ ❸ The courtyard garden of the Liebieghaus museum is a wonderfully tranquil spot. Good range of cakes. 🅐 Schaumainkai 71 🕓 11.00–20.00 Tues–Fri, 11.00–18.30 Sat, 10.00–20.00 Sun 🅝 U-Bahn: 1–3 to Schweizer Pl.; bus: 46 to Städel

Café Noah £ ❹ This bright yellow café offers tasty salads and great all-day breakfasts. 🅐 Affentorpl. 20 ☎ (069) 618 757 🕓 10.00–24.00 Mon–Sat 🅝 S-Bahn: 3–6 to Lokalbahnhof; bus: 30, 36 to Affentorpl.

Schiffercafé £ ❺ Tea and coffee in tasteful surroundings. Breakfast until 15.00. 🅐 Schifferstr. 36 🅦 www.schiffercafe.de 🕓 08.00–20.00 Mon–Fri, 08.00–19.00 Sat, 09.00–19.00 Sun 🅝 U-Bahn: 1–3 to Schweizer Pl.; bus: 46 to Schulstr.

Holbein's £–££ ❻ This café-restaurant at the Städel museum is a bit pricey, but the setting is unique. Good for lunch and dinner. 🅐 Holbeinstr. 1 ☎ (069) 6605 6666 🕓 10.00–24.00 Tues–Sun 🅝 U-Bahn: 1–3 to Schweizer Pl.; tram: 15, 16 to Otto-Hahn-Pl.

AFTER DARK

RESTAURANTS

Fichtekränzi £–££ ❼ Hearty local specialities at reasonable prices.
ⓐ Wallstr. 5 ❶ (069) 612 778 ⓦ www.fichtekraenzi.de ❸ 17.00–24.00
(kitchen closes 23.30) Ⓢ S-Bahn: 3–6 to Lokalbahnhof; bus: 30, 36
to Affentorpl.

Maaschanz ££ ❽ Delicious French cuisine at moderate prices.
Every month a different French province is featured on the menu.
ⓐ Färberstr. 75 ❶ (069) 622 886 ⓦ www.maaschanz.de

● Ebbelwei *comes in a stoneware jug and is served in a ribbed glass*

🕐 18.00–24.00 Tues–Sun (kitchen closes 23.00) Ⓝ U-Bahn: 4, 5 to Römer; bus 46 to Eiserner Steg

Maingau-Stuben, Hotel Maingau ££ ❾ Superb German regional cooking and excellent choice of German wines. ⓐ Schifferstr. 38–40 ⓣ (069) 610 752 Ⓦ www.maingau.de/restaurant 🕐 12.00–15.30, 18.00–01.00 Tues–Fri, 18.00–01.00 Sat (kitchen closes 22.00), 12.00–15.00 Sun Ⓝ U-Bahn: 1 3 to Schweizer Pl.; bus 46 to Schulstr.

Paolo's ££ ❿ With its delicious Italian food, Paolo's is a gift to night owls – the kitchen is open until four in the morning. ⓐ Schweizerstr. 1 ⓣ (069) 617 146 Ⓦ www.paolos.de 🕐 18.00–04.00 Ⓝ U-Bahn: 1–3 to Schweizer Pl.

Tandure ££ ⓫ Turkish restaurant. Try one of the specialities out of the *tandure* (clay oven). ⓐ Wallstr. 10 ⓣ (069) 612 543 Ⓦ www.tandure.com 🕐 12.00–15.00, 18.00–24.00 Ⓝ S-Bahn: 3–6 to Lokalbahnhof; bus: 30, 36 to Affentorpl.

BARS, CLUBS & DISCOS
Apfelweinwirtschaft Wagner A cider tavern frequented by both tourists and locals. Food served. ⓐ Schweizer Str. 71 🕐 11.00–24.00 Ⓝ U-Bahn: 1–3 to Schweizer Pl.

Dreikönigskeller Tiny basement club with great character and a vibrant live music scene from blues to surf, trash and swing. ⓐ Färberstr. 71 ⓣ (069) 6612 9804 Ⓦ www.dreikoenigskeller.com Ⓝ Bus: 30, 36 to Elizabethenstr. or 46 to Eiserner Steg

Stereobar Bar Retro design and cool sounds that bring the small dance floor to vibrant, sweaty life. ⓐ Abtsgässchen 7 ❶ (069) 617 116 ⓦ www.stereobar.de ⓛ 21.00–02.00 Thur & Sun, 22.00–03.00 Fri & Sat Ⓝ S-Bahn: 3–6 to Lokalbahnhof; bus: 30, 36 to Elisabethenstr.

Strandperle Especially in summer, when the tables spill outside, a great place to sip cocktails. ⓐ Shaumainkai, Eiserner Steg ❶ (069) 6032 5667 ⓦ www.strandperle-frankfurt.de ⓛ 15.00–02.00 Sun–Fri, 11.00–late Sat Ⓝ U-Bahn: 4, 5; tram: 11, 12 to Römer

Zum Eichkatzerl One of Frankfurt's oldest and most popular *Ebbelwei* taverns. Traditional German food, good atmosphere and great beer garden. Reservations recommended. ⓐ Dreieichstr. 29 ❶ (069) 617 480 ⓦ www.eichkatzerl.de ⓛ 16.00–24.00 Tues–Sun Ⓝ U-Bahn: 1–3 to Südbahnhof

Zum Feuerrädchen *Ebbelwei* tavern serving sparkling apple wine and beer as well as *Ebbelwei*. ⓐ Textorstr. 24 ❶ (069) 6657 5999 ⓛ 12.00–01.00 Ⓝ U-Bahn: 1–3 Frankfurt Süd

NIGHT-TIME WALKS & VIEWS
A stroll along Schaumainkai at night provides great views of the illuminated city skyline.

West of the Centre & Höchst

The main attractions in this part of town are the towering skyscrapers that make Frankfurt's skyline unique in Germany, a sprawling park that was once owned by one of Europe's wealthiest families, a fascinating natural history museum and the lovely old quarter of Höchst, with its many half-timbered buildings. You may be able to visit one of the trade fairs at the Messe, Europe's largest trade fair centre.

Though you can easily walk between sights like the Palmengarten and Senckenberg Museum, the U-Bahn or S-Bahn trains will save you time. Höchst is quickly reached by S-Bahn from the Hauptbahnhof.

SIGHTS & ATTRACTIONS

Altstadt Höchst

Around 10 km (6 miles) west of the city centre is the picturesque old quarter of Höchst. You'll find numerous half-timbered buildings, an intact medieval town wall, a Renaissance Schloss (castle) and the monumental Bolongaro Palace, a baroque building built by a wealthy Italian snuff manufacturer. Near the River Main is the 9th-century Justinuskirche, the oldest church in Frankfurt. Fine porcelain collections are on display in the Höchst Historical Museum and Dalberger House, the headquarters of Höchst Porcelain. A nice spot for a break after strolling the Altstadt's crooked, narrow streets is in one of the inviting cafés lining Schlossplatz. For the best panorama of town, take the passenger ferry to the opposite bank of the river.

Those who can manage it, should make an effort to visit Höchst during the annual four-week Höchster Schlossfest (Castle Festival), starting mid-June. The entire Altstadt comes to life with rock, jazz

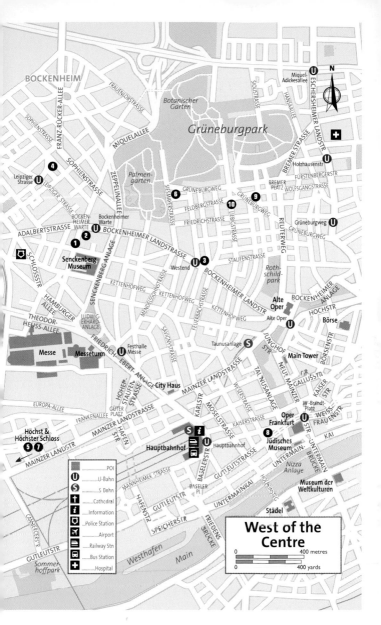

> ### STOLPERSTEINE (STUMBLING STONES)
> *Stolpersteine* are simple but poignant memorial plaques that commemorate the 10,000 or so Frankfurt Jews killed during the Nazi era. Set into the pavement in front of the houses where individuals lived before deportation to Hitler's death camps, the brass *Stolpersteine* record the person's name, date of birth, date of deportation and if known, date and place of death. The works are the idea of Cologne artist Gunter Demnig, who was awarded Germany's Federal Cross of Merit for the project. There are nearly 200 *Stolpersteine* in Frankfurt, many around Friedrichstrasse and Liebigstr.
> Ⓦ www.stolpersteine-frankfurt.de

and organ concerts, theatrical performances and, as a grand finale, a fireworks display. Ⓢ S-Bahn: 1, 2 to Höchst

Grüneburgpark
Grüneburgpark was once the private park of one of Frankfurt's wealthiest Jewish families, the Rothschilds. In 1935 the Nazis forced Albert Goldschmidt-Rothschild to sell the park to the city, and he later committed suicide in Swiss exile. Laid out in 19th-century English style, the 29 hectare (72 acre) park is one of the largest in the city and a favourite spot for joggers, skaters and those who just want to relax beneath the shade of 150-year-old trees. The Park Café, located in the neoclassical Schönhof Pavilion, is good for refreshments. Ⓐ August-Siebert-Str. Ⓣ (069) 598 969 Ⓒ 11.00–18.00, depending on weather Ⓤ U-Bahn: 6, 7 to Westend

Messe (Trade Fair grounds)

The northern entrance to the sprawling Trade Fair grounds is marked by Jonathan Borofsky's sculpture *The Hammering Man* and the pencil-shaped Messeturm (Trade Fair Tower). At 257 m (842 ft), and with 55 floors, this post-modernist skyscraper was the tallest building in Europe from 1991 to 1997, when it was eclipsed by Frankfurt's Commerzbank Tower. Other impressive structures include the post-modern Torhaus and the Festhalle (Festival Hall), once Europe's largest dome-roofed building and now the site of sporting events and rock concerts.

THE ROTHSCHILDS

This Jewish banking dynasty had its humble beginnings in Frankfurt's ghetto in the 18th century. Mayer Amschel Rothschild, the son of an itinerant moneylender, settled here in 1744 and was quickly able to establish himself in his father's profession. His five sons developed the family business into a financial force to be reckoned with. They established branches in several European capitals, and in an astonishingly short space of time, the Rothschild bank became the largest and most important financial institution in 19th-century Europe. The family lent money to kings and governments, financed railroads and the Suez Canal. The family amassed an incredible fortune and were richer in 19th-century terms than Bill Gates is today. The private Rothschild bank lost importance with the advent of big international banks in the 20th century. Today Rothschild banks still exist in London, Geneva and since 1989, after a long absence, again in Frankfurt.

FRANKFURT'S JEWISH COMMUNITY

With 7,000 members, Frankfurt has the third biggest Jewish community in Germany, but this is only a fraction of those living here before the Holocaust. In the 1930s Frankfurt's 30,000 Jews made up a fifth of the city's population. In 1945, only 602 remained. Even though it was set on fire, the **Westend synagogue** (ⓐ Freiherr vom-Stein-Str. 30 ⓘ (069) 726 263 ⏱ 10.00–17.00 Tues–Sun, 10.00–20.00 Wed Ⓜ U-Bahn: 6, 7 to Westend) was the only one in Germany to survive the anti-Jewish pogrom of *Kristallnacht*. Near the synagogue is Frankfurt's impressively designed **Frankfurt Jewish Community Centre** (ⓐ Savignystr. 66), which also has a kosher restaurant, Sohar (see page 25). See also the Jewish Museum, page 66.

Around 50 trade fairs take place here every year, a few of which are open to the public on certain days. They include the annual International Book Fair held in October, and the bi-annual International Motor Show, next on in September 2009 (see Annual events section on pages 10–11). ⓐ Ludwig-Erhard-Anlage 1 Ⓦ www.messe-frankfurt.com Ⓜ U-Bahn: 4; S-Bahn: 3–6; tram: 16, 17 to Messe

Palmengarten

Established in 1868, the hothouses of the Palmengarten contain one of Europe's largest and most attractive botanical collections. A stroll through the large Palmenhaus greenhouse, with its subtropical vegetation, is about as close to a jungle experience as you can get

⊙ *Palmengarten – an oasis among the skyscrapers*

in the city. There are also outdoor gardens, a lake and stages for theatrical performances and concerts. Annual events include the Rose and Light festival in June and Jazz im Palmengarten in August. Café Siesmayer is a good spot to relax after your visit.

ⓐ Palmengartenstr/ Siesmayerstr. 61 ⓣ (069) 2123 6689 ⓦ www.palmengarten-frankfurt.de ⓛ 09.00–16.00 Nov–Jan; 09.00–18.00 Feb–Oct ⓝ U-Bahn: 6, 7 to Palmengarten

CULTURE

Höchster Schloss (Höchst Palace)

The interior of the Renaissance Old Palace in Höchst, houses two museums. In the Hoechst AG Company Museum, you can learn about the history of the former Hoechst pharmaceutical company. For many years Hoechst AG played a vital role in the town's economic life, until in 1999 it was absorbed by the multinational Sanofi-Aventis. There is a fine collection of porcelain in the Historical Museum.

ⓐ Schlosspl. 16 ⓣ (069) 305 7366 ⓛ 10.00–16.00 Wed–Sun ⓝ S-Bahn: 1, 2 to Höchst

Kronberger Haus

The production of high-quality porcelain began in Höchst in 1746, making the firm Höchst Porcelain the third oldest manufacturer of porcelain in Europe after Dresden and Vienna. In Kronberger Haus you can view a collection of around 1,000 works of precious faïence and porcelain from the rococo and neoclassical periods. Also in the museum are paintings, a textile collection and a coin cabinet.

ⓐ Bolongarostr. 152 ⓣ (069) 2124 5474 ⓦ www.historisches-museum.frankfurt.de/kronbergerhaus ⓛ 11.00–18.00 Sat & Sun ⓝ S-Bahn: 1, 2 to Höchst

Senckenberg Museum

The *Tyrannosaurus Rex* in front of the museum gives away what makes this natural history museum so popular with kids and adults alike. Visit the Dinosaur Hall to be awed by examples from each major dinosaur group. Other displays include finds from the world famous Messel Fossil Pit, an anaconda swallowing a capybara, a fascinating section on human evolution, a mammal exhibition and a section devoted to crustaceans and spiders. As one of the largest and most important natural history museums in Europe, the Senckenberg will fascinate even those with only a passing interest in natural history. ⓐ Senckenberganlage 25 ⓣ (069) 75 420 ⓦ www.senckenberg.uni-frankfurt.de ⓛ 09.00–17.00 Mon, Tues, Thur & Fri, 09.00–20.00 Wed, 09.00–18.00 Sat & Sun ⓝ U-Bahn: 4, 6, 7; tram: 16 to Bockenheimer Warte

RETAIL THERAPY

Kaiserstrasse extends from the main railway station to the Hauptwache. Near the station are a few sex shops, interspersed with cafés and chic boutiques. Leipziger Strasse in Bockenheim has a diverse array of shops and restaurants.

The main food markets are the Bockenheimer Wochenmarkt (08.00–18.00 Thur) at Bockenheimer Warte and Kaisermarkt (09.00–19.00 Mon–Thur), a short stroll from the main railway station.

58's buy Heidt Exclusive designer labels for men and women. ⓐ Kronberger Str. 19 ⓣ (069) 725 535 ⓦ www.fiftyeights.de ⓛ 10.00–18.30 Mon–Wed, 11.00–20.00 Thur & Fri, 11.00–16.00 Sat

Alnatura Super Natur Markt Excellent range of organic food at refreshingly low prices. ⓐ Landgrafenstr. 11 ⓣ (069) 7953 4730 ⓦ www.alnatura.de ⓛ 08.00–19.00 Mon–Sat ⓤ U-Bahn: 4, 6, 7 to Bockenheimer Warte

Barbara Ochs Affordable haircuts for men and women in an impressive interior. Also manicures. ⓐ Leipziger Str. 5 ⓣ (069) 778 175 ⓦ www.ochs-friseure.de ⓛ 10.00–20.00 Mon–Thur, 09.00–20.00 Fri, 09.00–16.00 Sat ⓤ U-Bahn: 6, 7 to Leipziger Str.

🔽 *The Senckenberg Museum is a magnet for kids and adults alike*

Frauenbetriebe Design Leather handbags, chic clothing and reasonably priced jewellery. ❸ Leipziger Str. 11c ❶ (069) 707 3183 ❿ www.frauenbetriebe-online.de ◷ 10.00–19.00 Mon–Fri, 10.00–16.00 Sat ⓝ U-Bahn: 4, 6, 7 to Bockenheimer Warte

Ladengalerie Bockenheimer Warte Within a relatively small area, you'll find numerous cafés, restaurants, fashion shops, a bakery and a large supermarket. ❸ Bockenheimer Warte ⓝ U-Bahn: 6, 7 to Bockenheimer Warte

McTrek Budget-priced outdoor equipment, with good selection of brands such as Jack Wolfskin and North Face. ❸ Hamburger Allee 49–53 ❶ (069) 9799 2010 Ⓦ www.mctrek.de ❻ 10.00–19.00 Mon–Fri, 09.00–18.00 Sat ❷ S-Bahn: 3–6 to Frankfurt West

Parfümerie & Kosmetikinstitut Lehr Cosmetics and exotic scents by brands such as Chanel, Bulgari and Creed. ❸ Kaiserstr. 46 ❶ (069) 250 076 ❻ 09.30–19.00 Mon–Fri, 10.00–15.30 Sat ❷ U-Bahn: 4, 5; S-Bahn: 1–9 to Hauptbahnhof

Perlen und Schmuckcenter Westend A huge choice of pearl-studded jewellery, from dirt cheap to horrendously expensive. Also rings, necklaces and earrings in gold and silver. A good place for bargain-hunters. ❸ Friedrichstr. 23 ❶ (069) 717 172 Ⓦ www.perlen-schmuckcenter.de ❻ 10.00–18.00 Mon–Fri, 10.00–14.00 Sat ❷ U-Bahn: 6, 7 to Westend

Schmitt & Hahn International newspapers, magazines, postcards and maps. ❸ In Hauptbahnhof (main railway station) ❶ (069) 2425 2325 ❻ 04.30–24.00 Mon–Sat, 06.00–24.00 Sun ❷ U-Bahn: 4, 5; S-Bahn: 1–6, 8, 9; tram: 11, 12, 16, 17, 21

Thommy Stöber Run by a prize-winning hairstylist, this hairdressing salon offers exclusive coiffeurs and relaxing Ayurveda massage for your aching feet. ❸ Grüneburgweg 102 ❶ (069) 291 847 Ⓦ www.thommys.de ❻ 11.00–20.00 Tues–Thur, 09.00–20.00 Fri, 10.30–15.00 Sat ❷ U-Bahn: 6, 7 to Westend; bus: 36 to Simon-Bolivar-Anlage

Zambon International Bookshop with literature in numerous foreign languages. ❸ Kaiserstr. 55 ❶ (069) 252 914 Ⓦ www.zambon.net

🕒 10.00–19.00 Mon–Fri, 10.00–15.00 Sat 🔵 U-Bahn: 4, 5; S-Bahn: 1–6, 8, 9 to Hauptbahnhof

TAKING A BREAK

Café Albatros £ ❶ All-day breakfast and excellent-value buffet on Sundays and holidays. ⓐ Kiesstr. 27 ☎ (069) 707 2769 🕒 09.00–24.00 🔵 U-Bahn: 4, 6, 7 to Bockenheimer Warte

Café Extrablatt £ ❷ A student meeting point, with an 'all you can eat' buffet on Sundays. ⓐ Bockenheimer Landstr. 141 ☎ (069) 7940 3999 🕒 08.00–24.00 Mon–Thur, 08.00–01.00 Fri & Sat, 09.00–01.00 Sun 🔵 U-Bahn: 4, 6, 7 to Bockenheimer Warte

🔺 *Young Frankfurters hang out at the Café Extrablatt in Bockenheim*

Café Laumer £ ❸ Old-style café with a tradition stretching back to 1914. Great cakes. ❸ Bockenheimer Landstr. 67 ❶ (069) 727 912 Ⓦ www.cafe-laumer.de ⏰ 07.30–19.00 Mon–Sat, 09.00–19.00 Sun Ⓝ U-Bahn: 6, 7 to Westend

Café Paul £ ❹ Great atmosphere, tasty home-made cakes and excellent coffee (the beans come from a nearby roastery). The Italian owners make fresh pasta every Friday. ❸ Markgrafenstr. 19 ❶ (069) 7703 3717 ⏰ 10.00–23.00 Mon–Fri, 18.00–01.00 Sat Ⓝ U-Bahn: 6, 7 to Liepziger Str.

Café Wunderbar £ ❺ Popular for its mixed crowd, varied menu and good-value brunch on Sundays. ❸ Antoniterstr. 16 ⏰ 10.00–02.00 Ⓝ S-Bahn: 1, 2 to Höchst

Siesmayer £ ❻ Next to the Palmengarten, with a large terrace for enjoying cake and coffee outside. ❸ Siesmayerstr. 59 ❶ (069) 9002 9200 ⏰ 08.00–24.00 Ⓝ U-Bahn: 6, 7 to Bockenheimer Warte; bus: 36 to Siesmayerstr.

AFTER DARK

RESTAURANTS
Alte Zollwache £ ❼ Down-to-earth local food at a reasonable price. *Ebbelwei* is served along with beer and wine. ❸ Schlosspl., Höchst ❶ (069) 308 8035 Ⓦ www.alte-zollwache.de ⏰ 11.00–23.30 Ⓝ S-Bahn: 1, 2 to Höchst

Im Herzen Afrikas £ ❽ Sand on the floor and you eat with your fingers. Tasty chicken and lamb dishes from Eritrea. ❸ Gutleutstr. 13

⬥ *Relaxing at Alte Zollwache*

☎ (069) 2424 6080 🌐 www.im-herzen-afrikas.de 🕐 18.00–01.00
Ⓜ U-Bahn: 1–5 to Willy-Brandt-Pl.

Sushi King ££ ❾ Some of the best sushi in town, with friendly
service. ❸ Grünburgweg 81 ☎ (069) 7171 9877 🌐 www.fast-fresh-
fish.de 🕐 11.00–22.00 Ⓜ U-Bahn: 6, 7 to Westend

Gargantua ££–£££ ❿ Cosy interior and refined German cooking. The
chef is an ex-street fighter, ex-actor, popular columnist and cookbook
author. ❸ Liebigstr. 47 ☎ (069) 720 717 🌐 www.gargantua.de 🕐 12.00–
12.00, 18.00–21.30 Mon–Fri, 18.00–21.30 Sat Ⓜ U-Bahn: 6, 7 to Westend

BARS, CLUBS & DISCOS
Celcius Bar Popular student bar serving tasty snacks. ❸ Leipziger Str. 69
☎ (069) 707 2890 🌐 www.celsiusbar.de 🕐 18.00–02.00 Ⓜ U-Bahn:
6, 7 to Leipziger Str.

Bockenheimer Weinkontor Lovely hidden wine bar serving
a wide selection of wines and snacks. ⓐ Schlossstr. 92 (at the back)
ⓣ (069) 702 031 ⓦ www.bockenheimer-weinkontor.de ⓛ 19.00–01.00
Sun–Fri, 19.00–02.00 Sat ⓝ U-Bahn: 4, 6, 7 to Bockheimer Warte

Jimmy's Bar A classic bar serving superb drinks, with soft piano
music tinkling in the background. ⓐ Friedrich-Ebert-Anlage 40
ⓣ (069) 7540 2961 ⓛ 20.00 –04.00 ⓝ U-Bahn: 4, tram. 16, 17 to Messe

Main Tower Bar An upmarket 53rd-floor bar with amazing views.
Smart dress and reservations in the pricey restaurant required.
ⓐ Neue Mainzer Str. 52 ⓣ (069) 3650 4777 ⓦ www.maintower-
restaurant.de ⓛ 17.30 –01.00 Tues–Thur, 17.30–02.00 Fri & Sat
ⓝ U-Bahn: 6, 7 to Alte Oper; S-Bahn: 1–6, 8, 9 to Taunusanlage

Präsidium 19/11 Former police station, now one of the city's top discos.
ⓐ Friedrich-Ebert-Anlage 11 ⓣ (069) 7474 3978 ⓦ www.praesidium-1911.de
ⓛ 22.00–05.00 Fri & Sat ⓝ U-Bahn: 4, 5; S-Bahn: 1–9 to Hauptbahnhof

CINEMAS & THEATRES
English Theatre High-quality English-language drama and musicals.
ⓐ Kaiserstr. 34 ⓣ (069) 2423 1620 ⓦ www.english-theatre.org
ⓝ U-Bahn: 1–5 to Willy-Brandt-Pl.

Orfeo's Erben Ambitious international cinema, often in the original with
subtitles. The attached restaurant is very good. ⓐ Hamburger Allee 45
ⓣ (069) 7076 9100 ⓦ www.orfeos.de ⓛ Restaurant 12.00–15.00, 18.00–
01.00 Mon–Fri, 18.00–01.00 Sat & Sun ⓝ S-Bahn: 3–6 to Frankfurt West

▶ *Discover romantic castles like Eltville in the Rheingau*

Taunus

Sprinkled with picturesque towns and medieval castles, this attractive region of forest and hills spreads out to the north and west of Frankfurt. The area offers excellent walking and cycling along clearly marked trails, with restaurants catering to thirsty bikers and hikers at strategic points along the way. Individual attractions such as the Saalburg (Roman fort) and Hessenpark open-air museum can be reached by public transport from Frankfurt. Those who want to stay in the hills rather than in the city will find ample accommodation in Königstein or Bad Homburg, both linked to Frankfurt's public transport network.

SIGHTS & ATTRACTIONS

Bad Homburg

For the English aristocrats who frequented the elegant spa of Bad Homburg in the 19th century, the fresh air of the Taunus hills seemed like champagne and the expression *Champagnerluft* (champagne air) is still used. The lords and ladies also came for the healing qualities of the local thermal springs, and Bad Homburg was for many years the 'in' place to be.

These days ordinary folk can stroll through the beautiful spa park with its Thai temple, Russian chapel, casino and the exclusive spa complex of **Kaiser-Wilhelms-Bad** (Ⓦ www.kur-royal.de), where you can enjoy a full programme of beauty treatment in luxurious surroundings.

On the edge of the park is the **Taunus Therme** (Ⓦ www.taunus-therme.de), another wellness oasis with saunas, thermal waters, outdoor pools and more. Bad Homburg also boasts a 300-year-old baroque chateau, a summer residence for the last German Kaiser.
Tourist information ⓐ Kurhaus, Louisenstr. 56 ⓣ (06172) 178 110
Ⓦ www.bad-homburg.de ⓛ 08.30–18.30 Mon–Fri, 10.00–14.00 Sat

THE HOMBURG HAT

There is a story that while taking the waters in Bad Homburg, the British King Edward VII had a hat made according to his specifications by the hatter Möckel. The felt hat, with its narrow curled brim and a dent in the crown, became an instant success in well-to-do circles. Prominent Homburg hat wearers of the past include Anthony Eden, Winston Churchill and Dwight D. Eisenhower. Even today it is still worn by those with a taste for the exclusive.

⊗ S-Bahn: 5. Regular departures from Frankfurt Hauptbahnhof, journey takes 25 mins.

Grosser Feldberg

The highest peak in the Taunus hills at 880 m (2,887 ft), Grosser Feldberg is visited by around a million people a year. The views are fantastic, though on sunny summer weekends it can get crowded. There is a dense network of marked walking trails, making it easy to get away from the crowds to quieter peaks like the Kleiner Feldberg at 825 m (2,707 ft) and Altkönig at 798 m (2,618 ft). You can reach the peak by a combination of train and bus, or take the train to Königstein and walk from there (see Königstein). ⊗ Königstein-Bahn: 12 to Königstein from Frankfurt Hauptbahnhof, then bus 511. Journey takes just over an hour.

Königstein

Situated on the thickly wooded southern slopes of the Taunus hills, this small climatic health resort is one of the most picturesque

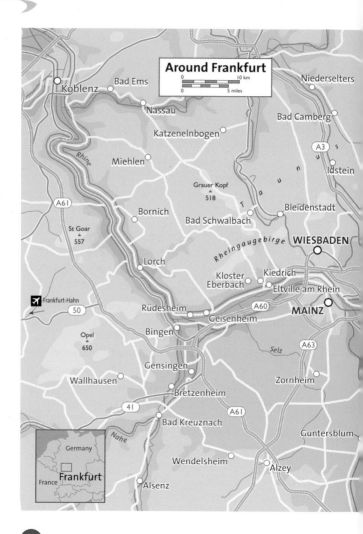

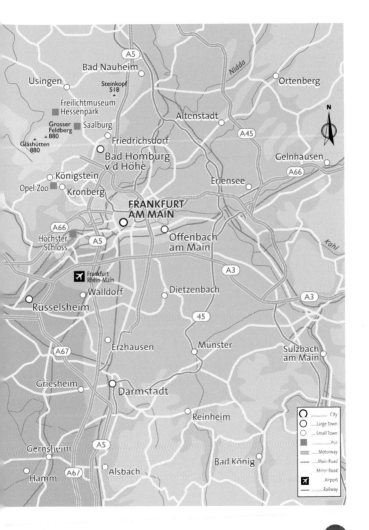

towns in the entire region. With its attractive *Kurpark* (spa park) and upmarket hotels and villas, Königstein is the destination of choice for Frankfurt's wealthy individuals.

A stroll through the beautifully preserved old town centre will bring you to the impressive ruins of Königstein Castle. Dating from the 13th century, it is Germany's second largest fortress complex. The view from the keep is breathtaking.

Take a look also at the Kirche St Marien (St Mary's Church) with its splendid rococo interior. There is an attractive restaurant in the *Kurpark*, with outdoor dining in summer.

Königstein is an excellent base for cycling or walking. Ask at the tourist office for bike hire. The Grosser Feldberg (see above) can be reached on foot in about two and a quarter hours and nearby Kronberg takes around one hour. Königstein's most interesting festival is the Burgfest (Castle Festival) in the first half of July.
Tourist office ❸ Hauptstr. 21 (Kurparkpassage) ❶ (06174) 202 251 ⓦ www.koenigstein.de ❶ 09.00–18.00 Mon, Tues, Thur & Fri, 09.00–12.00 Wed ❿ Königstein-Bahn: 12. Regular departures from Frankfurt Hauptbahnhof, journey takes 35 mins.

Kronberg

Like Königstein, the climatic health resort of Kronberg is also dominated by a 13th-century castle. Below it, you will find remnants of the medieval town wall and an *Altstadt* (old town) lined with half-timbered houses. Of the town's several churches, one of the most interesting is the so-called Streitkirche (Dispute Church), a church which was never completed due to a dispute between the local Catholics and Protestants. Also worth a look are the town's spacious parks and the nearby Opel-Zoo (see opposite). Schloss Friedrichshof, now a hotel, was once the residence of Victoria, consort of Kaiser Friedrich Wilhelm of

Germany and the eldest daughter of the British Queen Victoria.

Tourist office ✆ Katharinenstr. 7 ☎ (06173) 703 1400
🌐 www.kronberg.de 🕐 08.00–12.00 Mon & Tues, 08.00–12.00,
14.00–17.30 Wed, 07.00–12.00 Fri 🚊 S-Bahn: 4. Regular departures
from Frankfurt Hauptbahnhof, journey takes 20 mins.

Opel-Zoo

Near Kronberg, the Opel-Zoo holds around 1,200 animals, including
Europe's largest elephant herd, camels, hippos, giraffes, and tame

● *Breathe that healthy air in Königstein*

farmyard animals which the kids get to touch. Camel and pony rides are popular. Family restaurant. ⓐ Königsteiner Str. 35, Kronberg ⓣ (06173) 325 9030 ⓦ www.opelzoo.de ⓛ 09.00–18.00 (summer); 09.00–17.00 (winter) ⓢ S-Bahn: 4 to Kronberg from Frankfurt Hauptbahnhof, then bus 917 towards Falkenstein. Journey takes 25 mins.

CULTURE

Freilichtmuseum Hessenpark (Hesse open-air museum)

This large complex gives an impression of the architecture and historic life of rural communities throughout the state of Hesse. Over 100 buildings have been relocated and rebuilt on the site. Regular demonstrations of old crafts bring the place to life. The Market Square outside the main gate is free of charge and contains attractive historic houses, restaurants, souvenir shops and a hotel. ⓐ Laubweg 5, Neu-Anspach (northwest of Bad Homburg) ⓣ (06081) 5880 ⓦ www.hessenpark.de ⓛ 09.00–18.00 26 Feb–31 Oct ⓝ TaunusBahn (TSB): 15 from Frankfurt Hauptbahnhof, Wehrheim or Neu-Anspach, then bus 514 to the Hessenpark turnoff. Journey takes 1 hr. Admission charge

Saalburg

Reconstruction of a Roman fort which held around 600 soldiers in the 2nd century. Located on the Limes, a defensive wall that marked the border of the Roman Empire with the free Germanic tribes, it was eventually overrun around 259 AD. Within its turreted stone walls, you will find the commander's quarters, a granary, bread ovens and furnished rooms such as the regimental shrine and an officer's dining room. A tavern serves mock-Roman food and regular events help bring the past back to life. ⓐ Römerkastell Saalburg, Bad Homburg ⓣ (06175) 93740 ⓦ www.saalburgmuseum.de ⓛ 09.00–18.00

Mar–Oct; 09.00–16.00 Tues–Sun, closed Mon Nov–Feb ⓜ S-Bahn: 5 from Frankfurt to Bad Homburg, then bus 5 to Saalburg; TaunusBahn: 15 from Frankfurt Hauptbahnhof to Bahnhof Saalburg/Lochmühle. From there follow a signposted footpath to the Saalburg. Journey takes 40 mins to Bahnhof Saalburg, then 45 mins on foot.

RETAIL THERAPY

Bad Homburger Regio-Markt Hofgut Kronenhof Regional produce such as fruit, sausages, cheese, cakes, jams, fruit juices and beer from the Graf Zeppelin brewery. Large beer garden and restaurant on site. ⓐ Zeppelinstr. 10, Bad Homburg ⓣ (06172) 288 652 ⓦ www.badhomburger-brauhaus.de ⓛ 11.00–24.00

Freilichtmuseum Hessenpark The shops on the historic *Marktplatz* (marketplace) are open all year round. Here you can buy local food specialities such as Hessian sausages and home-baked German bread, along with traditionally dyed cloth, woven baskets, pottery and traditional Hessian country-style fashion. ⓐ Neu-Anspach (northwest of Bad Homburg) ⓣ (06081) 5880 ⓦ www.hessenpark.de

Homburger Hutsalon Rosemann Original Homburg and other exclusive handcrafted hats. ⓐ Rathausstr. 8, Bad Homburg ⓣ (06172) 24 340 ⓦ www.homburger-hutsalon.de ⓛ 09.00–13.00, 15.00–18.30 Mon, Tues, Thur & Fri, 09.00–13.00 Wed, 09.00–13.30 Sat

Konditorei-Café Kreiner Gift wrapped boxes of *Königstein-Pralinen* (filled chocolates) and other sweet treats. ⓐ Hauptstr. 10, Königstein ⓣ (06174) 1024 ⓦ www.cafe-kreiner.de ⓛ 09.30–18.00 Wed–Fri, 09.00–18.00 Sat, 10.00–18.00 Sun

Ladengalerie im Kurhaus Shopping gallery housing restaurants, exclusive fashion shops and more. ⓐ Louisenstr. 58, Bad Homburg Ⓦ www.kurhaus-ladengalerie.de

TAKING A BREAK

Café Kofler £ Great cakes in this café, open since 1823. ⓐ Audenstr. 2–4, Bad Homburg ⓣ (06172) 945 980 Ⓛ 08.00–19.00 Mon–Sat, 10.00–18.00 Sun

Kartoffel Küche £ Tasty, healthy potato-based dishes in a rustic setting. ⓐ Audenstr. 4, Bad Homburg ⓣ (06172) 21 500 Ⓦ www.restaurant-kartoffelkueche.de Ⓛ 12.00–14.00, 18.00–24.00

Villa Borgnis 'Kurhaus im Park' ££ Lovely Swiss-style villa with a large terrace for outdoor dining. Every 1st and 3rd Sunday of the month they serve a generous buffet brunch. ⓐ Hauptstr. 21, Königstein ⓣ (06174) 93 630 Ⓦ www.villaborgnis.de Ⓛ 10.00–23.00 Tues–Sat, 11.00–18.00 Sun

AFTER DARK

Louisen Lounge £ Wide range of cocktails and freshly made kebabs, falafels and salads, in the centre of Bad Homburg. ⓐ Louisenstr. 84b, Bad Homburg ⓣ (06172) 682 811 Ⓦ www.louisenlounge.de Ⓛ 10.00–01.00 Mon–Thur, 10.00–03.00 Fri & Sat

Restaurant Am Römerbrunnen ££ Mediterranean-style food in the restaurant and hearty local specialities in the beer garden. ⓐ Kisseleffstr. 27, Bad Homburg Ⓦ www.roemerbrunnen.de ⓣ (06172) 182 730 Ⓛ Bar 11.30–23.00, Kitchen 12.00–15.00, 18.00–23.00

Wilmenrod ££ Located in an attractive half-timbered building, the restaurant serves local cuisine with an international touch.
🅐 Limburger Str. 22, Königstein 🕿 (06174) 969 868
🆆 www.wilmenrod.de 🕓 18.00–01.00 (kitchen closes 23.00)

ACCOMMODATION

Gästehaus Villa Rosengarten £ Guesthouse next to the spa park and close to the main attractions. Rooms with kitchen facilities. Non-smokers only. 🅐 Im Rosengarten 8, Bad Homburg
🕿 (06172) 488 600 🆆 www.villa-rosengarten.de

Haus Villmer £ Comfortable guesthouse with self-contained holiday flats for those staying a week or longer. 🅐 Ölmühlweg 20, Königstein
🕿 (06174) 5544

Jugendherberge Haus Saalburg £ Youth hostel near the Bad Homburg Schloss, for families and individual travellers. A Youth Hostel Association or Hostelling International membership card is required. 🅐 Mühlweg 17, Bad Homburg 🕿 (06172) 23 950 🆆 www.djh-hessen.de

Hotel Haus am Park ££ Small, quiet hotel next to the spa park. Buffet breakfast included in price. Children welcome. 🅐 Paul-Ehrlich-Weg 3, Bad Homburg 🕿 (06172) 98 450 🆆 www.hotel-haus-am-park.de

Hotel Kronberger Hof ££ Pleasant small hotel and restaurant
🅐 Bleichstr. 12, Kronberg 🕿 (06173) 709 060 🆆 www.kronberger-hof.de

Hotel Sonnenhof £££ Picturesque hotel with all the comforts.
🅐 Falkensteiner Str. 9, Königstein 🕿 (06174) 29080

Rheingau

Vineyard-covered slopes producing some of the world's best Riesling wines, medieval castles and monasteries, charming half-timbered villages and boat trips on the River Rhine are just some of the ingredients that make this idyllic region so attractive. Easily reached by boat, car or train from Frankfurt, the Rheingau is worth more than just a day trip. There is an excellent range of accommodation in Eltville or Rüdesheim, and these wine-growing towns also offer numerous possibilities for buying and trying the local wine. This is the best place to enjoy a meal and wine in a traditional wine-grower's tavern.

SIGHTS & ATTRACTIONS

Eltville

Located directly on the Rhine, this lovely wine-growing town has an atmosphere like southern France. Stroll along the shady Rhine promenade or through the narrow cobbled streets of the Altstadt, where you will find some beautiful half-timbered buildings and a Gothic *Pfarrkirche* (parish church) with a richly furnished interior. The town has a 14th-century castle with a massive keep. The sun-drenched slopes behind Eltville produce wines and an excellent *Sekt* (sparkling wine). Don't miss the annual Sekt Festival on the first Sunday in July.

Tourist office ⓐ Rheingauer Str. 28 ⓣ (06123) 90 980 ⓦ www.eltville.de ⓛ 10.00–13.00, 14.00–18.00 Mon, Tues, Thur & Fri, 14.00–18.00 Wed, 10.00–13.00 Sat ⓥ Regional Express train from Frankfurt Hauptbahnhof to Eltville. Journey takes 50 mins.

Kloster Eberbach

Former 12th-century Cistercian monastery famed for its appearance in the film *The Name of the Rose*, starring Sean Connery. Eberbach looks back on over 800 years of wine-growing history and is today Germany's largest wine estate. You can buy top quality Riesling wines in the Vinothek, near the museum entrance, or sip it in one of the restaurants in the park grounds. During the Rheingau Music Festival in summer, concerts of classical music are often held within the monastery walls. In the surrounding woods are numerous waymarked trails.

Though it costs nothing to wander around the monastery grounds, it is worth having a look at the impressive interior. Stroll through the cloisters and visit the monastery church to see the beautifully sculpted medieval burial slabs. In the lay brothers' refectory are huge old wooden wine presses, and the early Gothic monks' dormitory has an impressive vaulted ceiling. ➌ Eltville (monastery is northwest of town near Kiedrich) ➊ (06723) 917 8115 Ⓦ www.klostereberbach.de 🕐 11.00–17.00 Ⓝ S-Bahn: 1 to Wiesbaden Hauptbahnhof, then Regional train to Eltville station. From here bus 5482 to Kloster Eberbach. Journey takes 1 hr 40 mins. Admission charge

River trips

A boat trip on the Rhine is one of the highlights of an excursion to the Rheingau. From the comfort of the deck you will see imposing castles, picturesque villages and vineyard-covered slopes. From Frankfurt, the Primus Fleet offers scenic trips to Rüdesheim with a two and a half hour stop on land. The boats depart from Frankfurt's Eiserner Steg (see page 78). Alternatively you can take the train directly to Rüdesheim, from where the Bingen-Rüdesheimer fleet offers regular sailings into the Rhine Valley.

STRAUSSWIRTSCHAFTEN

These traditional wine-growers' taverns are only open at certain times of the year, and enable the local wineries to serve their own wine, along with a meal, to paying guests – a privilege which goes back centuries. They are often identified by a *Strauss* (wreath) that hangs outside the entrance. Most of these taverns are much cheaper than normal restaurants, and you can be assured of good local wine and home cooking. Ask at the tourist office.

Two tips for Rüdesheim:

Weingut Jacob Lill ⓐ Im Rosengässchen ⓒ June–Sept, and **Weingut Franz Kunger** ⓐ Kellerstr. 14 ⓒ Oct–Jan

Bingen-Rüdesheimer ⓐ Rheinkai 10, Bingen ⓣ (06721) 14140 ⓦ www.bingen-ruedesheimer.com

Rüdesheim

This famous wine-growing town is one of the oldest centres of tourism in Germany. Stroll down Drosselgasse, a narrow alley packed with wine bars, restaurants and cramped souvenir shops, or slip into one of the back streets to discover half-timbered buildings and cosy restaurants run by local wine growers.

A popular excursion is to take a *Kabinenseilbahn* (cable car) over vineyard-clad slopes to the Niederwald Monument. This gigantic statue of Germania was erected following the Franco-Prussian War of 1870–71 to commemorate German unification under the Prussian Empire. There are breathtaking views over the Rhine Valley from the terrace and good walking through the surrounding woods. One walk leads west via Jagdschloss Niederwald, a hotel and upmarket restaurant, to where a chair-lift goes down to Assmannshausen – a small town with some picturesque corners and outstanding red wine. From you can walk back through the vineyards or to take a boat. Maps and sailing timetables are available from the tourist office in Rüdesheim.

The ruins of the 13th-century Ehrenfels Castle, to the west of town near Assmanshausen, can be reached on foot from Rüdesheim in roughly an hour.

Regular passenger and car ferries link Rüdesheim to Bingen, on the opposite bank of the Rhine. On the trip over you'll notice a yellow tower in the middle of the river, the 14th-century Mäuseturm (Mice Tower). There are good views from the terrace of Klopp Castle, directly above town. Bingen's Rhine promenade is landscaped as a park, with a lovely beer garden under the shade of huge trees.

The most spectacular of the many festivities in Rüdesheim is the Rhein im Feuerzauber in early July (ⓦ www.rhein-im-feuerzauber.de), a fireworks display timed to go off when a huge fleet of ships illuminated with Bengal lights sail by. This is best seen from Bingen. Other top festivities include the Weihnachtsmarkt (Christmas Fair), from the end of November to Christmas, and the Winzerfest (Wine Festival) in mid-August.

Tourist office ⓐ Geisenheimer Str. 22 ⓣ (06722) 19 433 ⓦ www.ruedesheim.de ⓛ 09.00–18.00 Mon–Fri, 10.00–17.00 Sat & Sun ⓡ Regional Express trains from Frankfurt Hauptbahnhof to Rüdesheim. Journey takes around an hour.

CULTURE

Kurfürstliche Burg Eltville

Built on the banks of the Rhine in 1330, this lovely castle used to be the seat of the bishops of Mainz. Today, it hosts a small exhibition devoted to the history of printing. Walk up to the castle from the Rhine to get a better idea of the moat system and ramparts once used to protect the castle. In summer, climb the 24m (79 ft) high tower for a small fee for a great view. ❸ On the Rhine, Eltville ● Grounds 09.30–19.00 Apr–Oct, 10.30–17.00 Nov–Mar, Tower 14.00–18.00 Fri, 11.00–18.00 Sat & Sun, Apr–Oct only

Museum für Weingeschichte (Wine History Museum)

With walls over 2 m (6 ft) thick, the 12th-century Brömserburg could withstand all attacks. Today this formidable defensive fortress houses the Rheingau Wine History Museum. There are over 2,000 wine-related exhibits on display, including drinking vessels from antiquity to the present day. The museum has a wine bar open on Saturdays and Sundays. ❸ Rheinstr. 2, Rüdesheim ❶ (06722) 2348 Ⓦ www.rheingauer-weinmuseum.de ● 10.00–18.00 mid-Mar–end Oct

Siegfried's Mechanisches Musikkabinett (Mechanical Music Museum)

Explore the fascinating world of self-playing mechanical musical instruments. Among the antique instruments on display is a self-playing concert piano from 1904. It was able to render classical music so well that it impressed even great piano virtuosos when first presented to the public. ❸ Brömserhof, Oberstr. 29, Rüdesheim ❶ (06722) 49 217 Ⓦ www.siegfrieds-musikkabinett.de ● 10.00–18.00 Mar–Dec

RETAIL THERAPY

Käthe Wohlfahrt Chain selling traditional German Christmas decorations, music boxes, cuckoo clocks, wooden nutcrackers and other souvenirs. ❸ Oberstr. 35, Rüdesheim ❶ (0986) 4090 ⓦ www.wohlfahrt.com ❶ 09.00–19.00 Mon–Sat, 09.00–18.00 Sun

BUYING WINE

There are numerous opportunities to buy white wines in the Rheingau region, the finest being the Rieslings. For red wine, try the *Spätburgunder* (Pinot Noir) wines, in particular those from Assmanshausen, near Rüdesheim. Though there are plenty of shops selling gift boxes with selected wines you can often get the best deals from the wine growers themselves. Most will let you taste the wine before you buy. Otherwise the local *Weinstuben* (wine bars) and *Strausswirtschaften* (see page 118) are great places to try with a meal or snack.

Abtei St Hildegard Located in the vineyards above Rüdesheim, the abbey produces some fine wines. Great views of the Rhine Valley from here too! ❸ Klosterweg, Rüdesheim ❶ (06722) 499 130 ⓦ www.abtei-st-hildegard.de ❶ 09.30–11.45, 14.00–17.00 Mon–Sat

Eltviller Vinothek Around 80 different wines, sparkling wines and spirits from local vineyards, at the same price as direct from an estate. ❸ Rheingauer Str. 38, Eltville ❶ (06123) 601 780 ⓦ www.eltviller vinothek.de ❶ 16.00–19.00 Mon–Thur, 12.00–19.00 Fri–Sun

Weingut Georg Breuer The cellars may be viewed for a fee, and the estate's vinothek has some excellent wines, such as the Rüdesheimer Schlossberg and Rauenthaler Nonnenberg. ❸ Grabenstr. 8, Rüdesheim ❶ (06722) 1027 ❿ www.georg-breuer.com ❺ 10.00–17.00

Weingut Dr Heinrich Nägler Wine has been grown on this estate by the same family for six generations. The main type is Riesling, but all wines carry the VDP seal of excellence. ❸ Friedrichstr. 22, Rüdesheim ❶ (06722) 2835 ❿ www.weingut-dr-naegler.de ❺ Sales 14.00–18.00

Weingut Freiherr Langwerth von Simmern The oldest family-run wine estate in Germany. Top wines and accessories plus a wine-tasting stall. ❸ Kirchgasse 6, Eltville ❶ (06123) 92 110 ❿ www.langwerth-von-simmern.de ❺ 09.00–12.00, 13.00–17.00 Mon–Fri, 10.00–17.00 Sat

TAKING A BREAK

Altstadtcafé Glockenhof £ One of the best places in town for cakes and coffee. Try the Eltviller Rosentörtchen tarts. ❸ Marktstr. 3 ❶ (06123) 61 141 Eltville ❺ 09.00–evening

Café in Hotel Felsenkeller £ Enjoy cake, coffee and meals on the sunny terrace under a huge Linden tree. ❸ Oberstr. 39 ❶ (06722) 94 250 ❺ 10.00–dark Mar–Nov

---

❿ Rüdesheim's wine alley, the Drosselgasse

Café Schwab £ A good selection of cakes and snacks in an old-fashioned atmosphere. ❷ Schwalbacher Str. 12, Eltville ❶ (06123) 2217 ❸ 09.00–18.30 Tues–Sat, 09.30–18.30 Sun

Gasthaus Winzerkeller £ Café and restaurant in a beautiful 17th-century house. ❷ Oberstr. 33, Rüdesheim ❶ (06722) 2324 Ⓦ www.winzerkeller.com ❸ 10.00–evening Mar–Dec

AFTER DARK

Hajo's Bierakademie and Disco Gnoom £ Hajo's is a pub in the style of the 20s, with occasional live music, while the 'Gnoom' (Gnome) is a popular disco. ❷ Rheinstr. 10, Rüdesheim Ⓦ www.hajos.de, www.gnoom.com ❸ Hajo's 18.00–02.00 Mon–Fri, 14.00–02.00 Sat & Sun, Gnoom 24.00–05.00 Fri & Sat

Zur Lindenau £ The oldest family-run wine house and restaurant in Rüdesheim. Down-to-earth regional food and of course, great wine. ❷ Löhrstr. 9 ❶ (06722) 3327 Ⓦ www.zur-lindenau.de ❸ 08.00–21.30

Gutsausschank Gelbes Haus ££ Situated in a lovely old house, this restaurant has a pleasant terrace with views over the Rhine. ❷ Burgstr. 3, Eltville ❶ (06123) 5170 ❸ 16.00–late Mon–Fri, 11.30–late Sat & Sun (kitchen closes 22.00)

Burg Crass £££ Upmarket restaurant in a castle with a beautiful location near the Rhine. ❷ Freygässchen 1, Eltville ❶ (06123) 975 110 ❸ 10.00–21.30 Ⓦ www.burgcrass-eltville.de

ACCOMMODATION

Campingplatz am Rhein £ Campsite with superb location close to the river and town. ⓐ Kastanienallee, Rüdesheim ⓣ (06722) 2528 ⓦ www.campingplatz-ruedesheim.de ⓛ end Apr–early Oct

Gästehaus Jensen £ Family-run guesthouse. Rooms with en suite or shared facilities. ⓐ Lönsweg 3, Eltville ⓣ (06123) 2485

Hotel Lindenwirt £ For the complete wine experience, sleep in one of the hotel's six giant wine barrels fitted out with bed and tiny bathroom. These special rooms are only available in summer, but the hotel's other 84 comfortable rooms are available all year round. ⓐ Drosselgasse, Rüdesheim ⓣ (06722) 9130 ⓦ www.lindenwirt.com

Weingut-Gästehaus Offenstein Erben £–££ Stay at a winery and enjoy a generous breakfast buffet with a glass of Sekt. ⓐ Holzstr. 14, Eltville ⓣ (06123) 2137 ⓦ www.offenstein-erben.de

Breuer's Rüdesheimer Schloss ££–£££ Imposing 18th-century building with modern comforts. ⓐ Steingasse 10, Rüdesheim ⓣ (06722) 90 500 ⓦ www.ruedesheimer-schloss.com

Wiesbaden & Mainz

These two small cities are quite different in character from Frankfurt and are separated from one another by the River Rhine. Both are capitals of their respective federal states; Wiesbaden of the state of Hesse (the same state as Frankfurt) and Mainz of neighbouring Rhineland-Palatinate (or Rheinland-Pfalz in German). Once known as 'Golden Mainz', due to its riches and the splendour of its architecture (largely destroyed in World War II), Mainz now prides itself on its magnificent cathedral, picturesque old quarter and on being the 'capital' of the Rhenish Carnival celebrations. Wiesbaden's attractions include its exclusive shops, a beautiful spa and the numerous old villas that can be seen in the vicinity of the Neroberg, a local hill.

WIESBADEN

SIGHTS & ATTRACTIONS
Tourist information ➌ Marktstr. 6 ❶ (0611) 1729 930
Ⓦ www.wiesbaden.de ⓛ 10.00–17.00 Mon–Fri, 10.00–17.00 Sat, 11.00–17.00 Sun Ⓢ S-Bahn: 1 from to Wiesbaden Hauptbahnhof. Journey takes 33 mins with the Regional train, and between 45–55 mins with the S-Bahn.

Altstadt
Wiesbaden's small old town centre can be reached from the railway station along Bahnhofstrasse. Focal point of the Altstadt is the Schlossplatz (Palace Square), with its 18th-century Marktbrunnen (Market Fountain). Fringing the square is the Alte Rathaus (Old Town Hall, 1610) and the Neue Rathaus (New Town Hall, 1887), the seat of

the city council. The late classical Stadtschloss (City Palace) was built in 1840 as a residence for the Duke of Nassau, and is now used by the Hessian state parliament. Perhaps the most striking building on the square is the red brick, neo-Gothic Marktkirche (Market Church) with its elegant spires. Built in the 19th century, its west tower reaches a height of 92 m (302 ft), making it the city's tallest building.

On the edge of the Altstadt (just off Langgasse) are remnants from the city's antique past. Next to the Römertor, a reconstructed Roman Gate, are fragments of the 4th-century AD Heidenmauer (Heathen's Wall). It formed part of a Roman stronghold and in the neighbouring open-air museum there are copies of finds made during excavations.

Kaiser-Friedrich-Therme

Built in 1913 and restored to its former splendour in 1999, this spa complex has a stunning interior. The beautiful Irish-Roman Bath is the centrepiece of the spa, with a cold-water swimming pool and a Russian and Finnish sauna among its various features. Massages and a selection of beauty treatments are also offered.
ⓐ Langgasse 38–40 ☏ (0611) 172 9660 Ⓦ www.wiesbaden.de/baeder Ⓛ 10.00–22.00 Sat–Thur, 10.00–24.00 Fri. Tues is for women only.

Kurhaus & Kurpark

After crossing the busy Wilhelmstrasse to the west of the Altstadt, a walk through a pleasant park will bring you past the Hessian State Theatre to the imposing Kurhaus. This building houses Wiesbaden's magnificently furnished casino, and its impressive interior is also a venue for important concerts of classical music. Behind the Kurhaus, the large landscaped park with its small lake is a great place to relax. Northwest of the Kurhaus, at the corner of Kranzplatz and Taunusstrasse,

is the Kochbrunnen (Hot Fountain). This fountain marks the spot where 15 of the city's 26 thermal springs meet. It's safe to drink from the fountain, but the mineral water is not to everyone's taste.

Neroberg

Rising behind Wiesbaden to a height of 245 m (804 ft), the hill known as the Neroberg offers spectacular views over the city and its surroundings. The NerobergBahn (cable car) saves you the trouble of an uphill walk. Near the upper terminus is a café serving light meals. A little further downhill from the summit you will find the Opelbad, an outdoor swimming pool with fantastic views over Wiesbaden. Also on the Neroberg is the Greek Chapel, as the 19th-century Russian Orthodox church is often called.

Schloss Freudenberg

Learn about natural phenomena such as gravity, light, darkness and sound by experiencing them in a fun way. The dark maze is one of the highlights of the interactive museum. ① (0611) 4110 141 ⓦ www.schlossfreudenberg.de ① 09.00–18.00 Tues–Fri, Mar–Oct; 09.00–17.00 Tues–Fri, Nov–Feb; 12.00–18.00 Sat & Sun ② Bus: 4, 14, 27 to Platz der Deutschen Einheit, then bus 23 or 24 to Märchenland. Journey takes 30 mins.

CULTURE

Museum Wiesbaden

Contains an outstanding collection of works by the Russian Expressionist artist Alexei von Jawlensky (1864–1941). Also regular exhibitions of contemporary art.

▶ *It's a fun ride up to the Neroberg*

ⓐ Friedrich-Ebert-Allee 2, Wiesbaden ① (0611) 335 2250
ⓦ www.museum-wiesbaden.de ⓛ 10.00–20.00 Thur–Sat & Tues,
10.00–17.00 Wed & Sun

RETAIL THERAPY

In Wiesbaden, exclusive shops selling designer clothing, furniture
and jewellery are found along Wilhelmstrasse and in the area
around Burgstrasse and Webergasse, the so-called Quellenviertel
(Hot Springs District). For high-quality antiques check Taunusstrasse.
Those looking for more down to earth shopping will find plenty of
choice along Kirchgasse, Langgasse and around the Altstadt. The
Wiesbadener Wochenmarkt (Farmers' Market) is held near the Neue
Rathaus every Wednesday and Saturday from 07.00 until 14.00.

TAKING A BREAK

Café Blum £ Good for a light lunch and the cakes are in a class
of their own. ⓐ Wilhelmstr. 46, Wiesbaden ① (0611) 300 007
ⓛ 08.00–19.00 Mon–Fri, 09.00–19.00 Sat & Sun

Der Turm £ On the Neroberg with fantastic views over Wiesbaden.
Good, simple bistro style food. ⓐ Neroberg 1, Wiesbaden
① (0611) 959 0987 ⓛ 12.00–24.00

Lumen ££ Enjoy the sunshine on the large terrace, filled with
sand and deckchairs in summer. The menu offers plenty of choice.
ⓐ Dernsches Gelände, Wiesbaden ① (0611) 300 200 ⓦ www.lumen-
wiesbaden.de ⓛ 09.00–01.00 Mon–Thur, 09.00–02.00 Fri & Sat,
10.00–01.00 Sun

AFTER DARK

C/O Lounge ££ This atmospheric lounge bar is a great place to chill out. Alternating DJs Thur–Sat and a great courtyard for summer nights. ⓐ Moritzstr. 52 ⓣ (0611) 901 8970 ⓦ www.co-lounge.de ⓛ 18.00–01.00 Sun–Thur, 18.00–02.00 Fri & Sat

Weinhaus Kögler ££ Wiesbaden's oldest wine house, serving primarily wines from the Rheingau region alongside regional specialities. ⓐ Grabenstr. 18 ⓣ (0611) 376 737 ⓦ www.weinhaus-koegler.de ⓛ 17.00–late Mon–Fri, 12.00–late Sat (summer); 17.00–late Mon–Sat (winter)

Hessisches Staatstheater Top-rate performances of opera, ballet and drama draw the crowds. ⓐ Christian-Zais-Str. 3, Wiesbaden ⓣ (0611) 1321 ⓦ www.staatstheater-wiesbaden.de

ACCOMMODATION

Aurora £ Quiet, central location with buffet breakfast included. ⓐ Untere Albrechtsstr. 9, Wiesbaden ⓣ (0611) 373 728 ⓦ www.aurora-online.de

Jugendherberge Wiesbaden £ The youth hostel is situated to the west of the town centre. A Youth Hostel Association or Hostelling International membership card is required. ⓐ Blücherstr. 66, Wiesbaden ⓣ (0611) 48 657 ⓦ www.djh-hessen.de

Bed & Breakfast In Der Villa ££ Sleep in style in this beautiful brick villa from 1898. A 15-min walk to town. ⓐ Weinbergstr. 6, Wiesbaden ⓣ (0611) 523 374 ⓦ www.bed-and-breakfast-wiesbaden.de

Trüffel ££ This small and stylish hotel with modern furnishings also has a good restaurant attached. ⓐ Webergasse 6–8 ⓣ (0611) 990 550 ⓦ www.trueffel.net

MAINZ

SIGHTS & ATTRACTIONS

Verkehrsverein Mainz (Tourist office) ⓐ Brückenturm am Rathaus ⓣ (06131) 286 210 ⓦ www.info-mainz.de ⓛ 10.00–18.00 Mon–Fri, 11.00–17.00 Sat ⓝ S-Bahn: 8 to Mainz Hauptbahnhof. Journey takes 33 mins on the IC train, 41 minutes on the S-Bahn.

Altstadt (Old town)

The **Dom St Martin** (St Martin's Cathedral) is about a 20-minute walk from the railway station. Over a 1,000 years old, this monumental cathedral ranks with those in Speyer and Worms as one of the most outstanding examples of Romanesque architecture in the whole of Germany. On the north side of the cathedral is a broad marketplace, lined with cafés and with an ornately decorated Renaissance Marktbrunnen on its eastern edge. Heading south around the Dom, Schöfferstrasse will bring you deeper into the city's pedestrianised old quarter. One of the prettiest ensembles of half-timbered buildings can be found on Kirschgarten, just off Augustiner Strasse. Further exploration of the Altstadt's crooked, narrow alleys will reveal more picturesque corners, while numerous inviting cafés provide a good excuse for a break.

Rheinufer

To get to the Rhine Embankment from the Altstadt continue south along Augustinerstrasse, pass the Church of St Ignatz on

Kapuzinerstrasse, then turn left through the narrow Hänleingässchen. Cross the busy Rheinstrasse and walk through the Fort Malakoff shopping complex.

On the other side of Fort Malakoff is a huge terrace opening onto the River Rhine. As well as an Italian restaurant with great views over the river, several beer gardens can be also be found here in summer. Cross the small bridge to the Victor Hugo Embankment and you can stroll through the riverside park, which on weekends is alive with joggers, skaters and picnicking locals. On a warm summer's evening it's great to just sit on the grass and watch the boats and the world go by. But if you want to be on a boat, you'll have to walk back north from the Malakoff Terrasse to where the boats of the Köln-Düsseldorfer (❶ (06131) 232 800 ❽ www.k-d.com) and Primus (❶ (069) 133 8370 ❽ www.primus-linie.de) fleets dock.

CULTURE

Dom (Cathedral) & museum

The cathedral's vast interior is indicative of the power and wealth that the archdiocese of Mainz once commanded, as is its monumental exterior. Of particular interest are the gravestones of the archbishops, the Romanesque St Gotthard's Chapel and the late Gothic cloister. The cathedral museum contains numerous works of priceless art acquired over the centuries. Cathedral ❸ Markt 10, Mainz ❶ (06131) 253 412 ❺ 09.00–18.30 Mon–Sun. Museum ❸ Domstr. 3 ❺ 10.00–17.00 Tues–Sun

Gutenberg-Museum

Johannes Gutenberg invented the printing press with moveable type, around 1440 in Mainz – an innovation comparable in its effect to the advent of the internet at the end of the 20th century. The city

has honoured its illustrious son with a museum dedicated to the history of printing. Pride of place among the exhibits goes to two original copies of the world-famous Gutenberg bible. A reconstruction of Gutenberg's workshop, along with demonstrations of old printing techniques, give a fascinating insight into the beginnings of the age of mass communication. ❷ Liebfrauenpl. 5, Mainz ❶ (06131) 1226 4044 ⓦ www.gutenberg-museum.de ❸ 09.00–17.00 Tues–Sat, 11.00–15.00 Sun

Museum für Antike Schifffahrt (Ancient Maritime Museum)

The highlights of this museum devoted to ancient shipbuilding are the models of two military boats from the Roman Rhine fleet, rebuilt at a scale of 1:10. The models are based on five wrecks that were discovered during the 1981–82 excavations for an extension of the Hilton Hotel in Mainz. Archaeologists believe these military ships were abandoned after a catastrophic defeat of the Roman Rhine army by invading Germanic tribes in 407 AD. Windows in the museum workshop allow you to view ongoing restoration work. ❷ Neutorstr. 2b, Mainz ❶ (06131) 286 630 ❸ 10.00–18.00 Tues–Sun

Römisch-Germanisches Zentralmuseum (Roman-Germanic Museum)

An important research institute and restoration centre, the museum has three permanent collections focusing on prehistory, the Roman period and the early Middle Ages. Combined they offer a unique overview of the prehistory and early history of Europe, the Near East and Egypt. The exhibits in the Roman section are of particular interest because Mainz itself is literally sitting on the remains of its Roman past, as excavations for a new shopping centre have proved. ❷ Kurfürstliches Schloss, Ernst Ludwig Pl. 2, Mainz ❶ (06131) 91 240 ⓦ www.rgzm.de ❸ 10.00–18.00 Tues–Sun

Stefanskirche (St Stephen's Church)

The main attraction of the Gothic Church of St Stephen is the stained-glass windows by the Russian-Jewish artist Marc Chagall. Although already in his nineties when he began work in the late 70s, the artist was able to create nine windows for the church before his death in 1985. They stand as a symbol of the bond

The Altstadt in Mainz invites you to take a break

between the Jewish and Christian faiths. Also worth seeing is the Gothic cloister. ⓐ Kleine Weissgasse 12, Mainz ⓣ (06131) 231 640 ⓛ 10.00–12.00, 15.00–17.00 Mon–Fri

RETAIL THERAPY

Shopping in the centre of Mainz is made pleasant by pedestrian zones such as the City-Meile, the area of shops between Ludwigsstrasse and Grosse Bleiche. Here you will find bookshops, large department stores, fashion shops and more besides. Also good for shopping is Grosse Bleiche, Am Brand and the Altstadt area. The latter offers a good variety of small shops offering such things as art, outdoor clothing, exclusive hats and jewellery. The city's main food market takes place in front of the cathedral on Tuesdays, Fridays and Saturdays. It is a lively affair and well worth a visit.

TAKING A BREAK

Alex £ The tables outside are good for people-watching while sipping your coffee. ⓐ Gutenbergpl. 14, Mainz ⓣ (06131) 144 7350 ⓛ 08.00–01.00 Mon–Thur, 08.00–03.00 Fri & Sat, 09.00–01.00 Sun

Augustinerkeller £ The rustic interior fits with the Altstadt, where it's located. Try the *Flammkuchen* (a speciality of neighbouring Alsace) as an alternative to the hearty German fare. ⓐ Augustinerstr. 26, Mainz ⓣ (06131) 222 662 ⓛ 12.00–23.00

Bagatelle £ With a relaxed mixed crowd, this café, located between the central station and the Rhine, has a student feel and good breakfasts. ⓐ Gartenfeldstr. 22, Mainz Neustadt ⓣ (06131) 612 050 ⓛ 09.00–01.00 Mon–Thur & Sun, 09.00–02.00 Fri & Sat

Café Grünewald £ Breakfast or lunch with a fantastic view of the cathedral. Located on the upper floor of Wehmeyer's fashion shop. On sunny days, the terrace stays open until later. ⓐ Am Höfchen 1, Mainz ⓣ (06131) 221 186 ⓛ 08.00–20.30 Mon–Fri, 08.00–17.00 Sat, 10.00–18.00 Sun

AFTER DARK

Biergarten auf der Mole £ Walk south 10 mins down the Rhine to find one of the most popular places in Mainz. Beer, sausages and chips is the standard fare. ⓐ Am Winterhafen

Eisgrub-Bräu £ The beer is brewed on the premises and the food is good and cheap. Very popular place in the evenings. ⓐ Weissliliengasse 1a, Mainz ⓣ (06131) 221 104 ⓛ 09.00–01.00 Mon–Thur, 09.00–02.00 Sat & Sun ⓦ www.eisgrub.de

Heiliggeist ££ Dine under a 13th-century vaulted ceiling – the interior alone makes this place worth a visit. ⓐ Mailandsgasse 11, Mainz ⓣ (06131) 225 757 ⓛ 16.00–01.00 Mon–Thur, 09.00–02.00 Fri–Sun ⓦ www.heiliggeist-mainz.de

Frankfurter Hof Venue for concerts ranging from classical to jazz. ⓐ Augustinerstr. 55, Mainz ⓣ (06131) 220 438 ⓦ www.frankfurter-hof-mainz.de

Staatstheater Mainz Recently refurbished, the State Theatre has superb acoustics for a varied programme of opera, concerts and ballet. ⓐ Gutenbergpl. 7, Mainz ⓣ Tickets (06131) 285 1222 ⓦ www.staatstheater-mainz.de

ACCOMMODATION

Jugendgästehaus Mainz £ This large youth hostel is located outside the centre in the district of Weisenau. A Youth Hostel Association or Hostelling International membership card is required. **ⓐ** Otto-Brunfels-Schneise 4 **ⓣ** (06131) 85 332 **ⓦ** www.diejugendherbergen.de/jugendherberge-mainz

Hotel Stadt Coblenz £ Reasonably priced hotel with a central location. **ⓐ** Rheinstr. 47–49, Mainz **ⓣ** (06131) 629 0444 **ⓦ** www.info-mainz.de/stadtcoblenz

Hotel Schwan ££ Historic hotel with attractive rooms and an attached restaurant. **ⓐ** Liebfrauenpl. 7, Mainz **ⓣ** (06131) 144920 **ⓦ** www.mainz-hotel-schwan.de

ⓓ *Rail is a comfortable way to reach Frankfurt and you can see a lot en route*

Directory

GETTING THERE
By air

For a short stay, those coming from the UK will find flying the quickest and most convenient way to get to Frankfurt. The main entry point is Frankfurt Rhein-Main Airport (☎ (01805) 372 4636), which is served by just about every major airline in the world.

Visitors from the UK and Ireland who travel with low-cost airline **Ryanair** (☎ 0906 270 5655 ⓦ www.ryanair.com) from London Stansted and Glasgow Prestwick fly to Frankfurt-Hahn Airport (☎ (06543) 509 200), roughly 125 km (78 miles) west of the city.

Average flying time is one and a half hours from London, seven and a half hours from New York. See pages 48–9 for more details on airports.

Many people are aware that air travel emits CO_2, which contributes to climate change. You may be interested in the possibility of lessening the environmental impact of your flight through Climate Care, which offsets your CO_2 by funding environmental projects around the world. Visit ⓦ www.climatecare.org

By road

The German *Autobahn* (motorway) system is well integrated into the European road network, with motorways converging on Frankfurt from all directions. The trip from London to Frankfurt via Dover, Ostend, Brussels, Cologne and Mainz takes roughly nine hours. The total distance is around 745 km (463 miles). The 50 km (31 mile) journey between Britain and France via the Channel Tunnel takes 35 mins. Times on the various ferry links between Dover and Calais range between 55 mins and one and a half hours. To choose the route best suited to you, visit ViaMichelin (Ⓦ www.viamichelin.co.uk) or the AA Route Planner Europe (Ⓦ www.theaa.com). For Channel Tunnel and ferry bookings see Ⓦ www.directferries.co.uk

Long-distance buses connect Frankfurt with most European countries, arriving at the Hauptbahnhof. From London by National Express the fastest journey time is about 15 and a half hours. Ⓦ www.nationalexpress.com

By rail

There are fast and comfortable connections to Frankfurt from London's Waterloo International station with the Eurostar. Change

🔽 *Trains from all over Europe converge at the Hauptbahnhof*

at Brussels (from Bruxelles-Midi EST station to Bruxelles-Midi), and from here the high-speed ICE train takes you direct via Achen and Cologne (Köln) to Frankfurt's Hauptbahnhof. Total journey time is about eight hours.

Alternatively, the TGV high-speed bullet train takes four hours from Paris to Frankfurt.

The monthly *Thomas Cook European Rail Timetable* has up-to-date schedules for European international and national train services.
Eurostar reservations (UK) ☎ 08705 186 186 ⓦ www.eurostar.com
Thomas Cook European Rail Timetable ☎ (UK) 01733 416477;
(USA) 1 800 322 3834 ⓦ www.thomascookpublishing.com

Package deals

Package deals (including hotels, rental car, etc) save you having to organise everything yourself and are often available at bargain prices. Many travel agents offer packages for 'weekend city escapes', as do airlines such as Ryanair. A good website to check for Frankfurt packages is ⓦ www.activitybreaks.com. The Frankfurt tourist office has a number of interesting packages for some of the city's major events, including the Christmas Market, special art exhibitions and sports events.
Frankfurt tourist office ☎ (069) 2123 8800 ⓦ www.frankfurt-tourismus.de

ENTRY FORMALITIES
Passport and visa requirements

Visas are not required by citizens of the USA, Canada, Republic of Ireland, Australia, New Zealand, the UK and members of other EU countries for visits of less than three months. South African nationals do require a visa. Citizens of the UK and of all countries except other EU states require a valid passport. EU citizens need only a national identity card.

Customs

There are no customs controls at borders for visitors from EU countries. Visitors from EU countries can bring in, or take out, goods without any restrictions on quantity or value, as long as these goods are for personal use only. Visitors from outside the EU are subject to restrictions. Most personal effects and the following items are duty-free: a portable typewriter; one video camera or two still cameras with ten rolls of film each; a portable radio, tape recorder, and laptop computer, provided they show signs of use; 400 cigarettes or 50 cigars or 250 g (9 oz) of tobacco; two litres (0.52 gallons) of wine or one litre (0.26 gallons) of liquor per person over 17 years old; fishing gear; one bicycle; skis; tennis or squash racquets; golf clubs.

As entry requirements and customs regulations are subject to change, you should always check the current situation with your local travel agent, airline or a German embassy or consulate before you leave. For current information on visas and customs requirements contact the Auswärtiges Amt (German Department of Foreign Affairs) ⓦ www.auswaertiges-amt.de

MONEY

The euro (€) is the official currency in Germany. €1 = 100 cents. It comes in notes of €5, €10, €20, €50, €100, €200 and €500. Coins are in denominations of €1 and €2, and 1, 2, 5, 10, 20 and 50 cents.

ATM (*Geldautomat*) machines are readily found at airports, railway stations, shopping centres and in downtown areas. They are the quickest and most convenient way to obtain cash. Instructions on use are available in English and other major European languages.

As well as in downtown areas, there are banks or bureaux de change at airports and main railway stations in the cities.

The most widely accepted credit cards are Eurocard and Mastercard, though other major credit cards such as Visa and American Express are also commonly accepted. Note that many supermarkets, smaller shops, restaurants, *pensions* (B&Bs) and other businesses, especially outside Frankfurt, do not accept credit or debit cards. It is advisable to always carry some cash along with your credit card.

Traveller's cheques are best cashed at a *Wechselbüro* (exchange bureau), because many banks won't change them.

HEALTH, SAFETY & CRIME

It is not necessary to take any special health precautions while staying in Frankfurt and the Rhein-Main region. Tap water is safe to drink, but do not drink water from lakes or streams in the surrounding countryside. Many Germans prefer *Mineralwasser* (bottled mineral water).

If you go walking in forested areas be careful of ticks. These blood-sucking parasites can transmit dangerous viral infections, along with various bacterial diseases. A good deterrent is the insecticide *permethrin*, sprinkled over your clothes. Avoid walking through long grass with bare legs. In any case, after a walk always check your body for ticks. If you find one remove it immediately with a pair of *Zeckenzange* (tick tweezers). These can be bought at pharmacies. If a rash develops from a bite, consult a doctor immediately.

Apotheken (pharmacies) can be recognised by a green-cross sign and are well-stocked, with expert staff.

German health care is of a very high standard, but it is not free. In most cases your health insurance should provide the coverage you need.

As in any big city, crime is a fact of life in Frankfurt. However, if you exercise the same care that you would at home, you should not have any special problems. Never leave valuables lying openly in your car, and always lock it. Strolling about the inner city at night is fairly safe, but avoid dimly lit streets. The areas around the Konstablerwache and main railway station have a problem with drug dealers, but regular police patrols tend to keep them in check. See also Emergencies section pages 152–3.

OPENING HOURS

Banks are usually open 08.00–13.00, 14.00–16.00 Mon–Fri (often until 17.30 Thur). With the exception of the Postbank inside post offices, which is open 08.00–12.00 Sat, banks remain closed on Saturdays and Sundays. Exchange bureaux at airports and main railway stations are usually open 06.00–22.00. ATMs are accessible 24 hours.

Post offices are usually open 08.00–18.00 Mon–Fri, 08.00–12.00 Sat. At airports and main railway stations in large towns and cities they often stay open longer. Post offices can also change currency.

Germany deregulated store opening hours in 2007, and many stores could be open later than the times given. In general, most supermarkets are open from 08.00–20.00 Mon–Sat. Other stores tend to open around 10.00 and close between 18.00 and 20.00. Expect many small shops to be closed on Saturday afternoon. All of the city's shops are closed on Sundays, except for bakeries, which open Sunday mornings, and kiosks. Most museums are normally open 09.00–18.00 Tues- Sun and only open on a Monday if a public holiday.

TOILETS

At airports, railway stations, U-Bahn and S-Bahn stations, you should not have a problem finding toilets. Otherwise, public toilets are spread rather thinly around the city. Most locals resort to using the facilities at cafés, restaurants and bars, though using them may not be appreciated if you are not a customer.

The cleanest public toilets are those with an attendant, who expects a small tip. Another good bet for a clean loo are the toilets at museums. Women's toilets are often marked with the usual pictograms, but if not, an 'F' is for *Frauen* (ladies), and an 'H' means *Herren*, (gentlemen). Public toilets suitable for wheelchairs are located at the U-Bahn station Hauptwache (🕒 07.15–22.00) and at the U-Bahn station Messe (🅐 Ludwig-Erhard-Anlage 1 🕒 07.00–22.00).

CHILDREN

Germany is generally a child-friendly place and no special health precautions need be taken. Most restaurants welcome children, and some have play corners for the kids. There is usually a kid's menu and if you ask, the staff will often be able to supply your children with pencils and paper at the table.

Nappies and other baby articles are readily obtained from supermarkets, *apotheken* (pharmacies) or a *drogerie* (drugstore selling various articles, but without prescription medications).

For child-friendly attractions, try the Frankfurter Zoo (see page 61) and the **Kindermuseum des Historischen Museums** (Museum for Children 🅐 Saalgasse 19 🌐 http://kindermuseum.frankfurt.de 🕒 10.00–18.00 Tues, Thur & Sun, 10.00–21.00 Wed 🅝 U-Bahn: 4, 5 to Römer) where children can actually touch and explore the exhibits. On the last Sunday of every month from 14.30–16.30, the Colonial Store is open for the kids to play shop.

There are numerous outdoor and indoor swimming pools in and around Frankfurt. They include the **Brentanobad** (Ⓝ U-Bahn: 6 to Am Fischstein) and Rebstockbad (Ⓝ Tram: 17 to Rebstockbad). For more details on these and other pools contact the tourist office. For a child-friendly café try **Zebulon-Spielcafé** (Ⓐ Grempstr. 23, Frankfurt ① (069) 773 554 Ⓛ 15.00–18.00 Ⓝ U-Bahn: 6 or 7 to Kirchpl.). Kids can go crazy in the playroom, while their parents relax with coffee and cakes.

COMMUNICATION
Internet
Internet access is provided by some libraries and internet cafés around the city. Try **CyberRyder** Ⓐ Töngesgasse 31 Ⓝ U-Bahn: 1–3, 6, 7 to Hauptwache, or **Saturn Internetcafé** Ⓐ Berger Str. 125–129 Ⓝ U-Bahn: 6 to Höhenstr.

Phone
Most public phones are card-operated. *Telefonkarten* (telephone cards) can be bought at any post office and some shops such as bookshops or kiosks at railway stations. A display shows how much credit is left. Instructions on how to use public telephones are written in English in phone booths for international calls. Otherwise, lift up the receiver, insert the telephone card and dial the number.

When making an international call, dial the access code 00, the international code you require, then drop the initial zero of the area code you are ringing. The international dialling code for calls from Germany to Australia is 61, to the UK 44, to the Irish Republic 353, to South Africa 27, to New Zealand 64, and to the USA and Canada 1.

The code for dialling to Germany from abroad, after the access code (00 in most countries) is 49. To call Frankfurt from abroad, the

code is 49 69. To call Frankfurt from within Germany dial 069 and then the number. If calling from Frankfurt itself, there is no need to dial 069.

Post

Postal services are quick and efficient. There are post offices at the airport, main railway station and on the Zeil in downtown Frankfurt. Stamps can be bought at the post offices or from automatic vending machines outside post offices. Postboxes are yellow. A standard airmail letter of up to 20g costs 70 cents within Europe and to the UK, and €1.70 to other international destinations. Postcards within Europe and to the UK cost 65 cents, other destinations €1.

ELECTRICITY

The supply nationally is 220 volts (AC), 50 Hertz. Round-ended, two-pronged adapters are needed for UK and USA appliances.

TRAVELLERS WITH DISABILITIES

Facilities for visitors with disabilities are generally quite good in Germany. They are usually indicated by a blue pictogram of a person in a wheelchair. In all towns and cities there are reserved car parks for people in wheelchairs, and motorway service stops, airports and main railway stations always have suitable toilet facilities. Most trains also have toilets accessible for wheelchairs.

Many cinemas, theatres and all important museums and public buildings are accessible for wheelchair users, as are many of Frankfurt's hotels. For further advice contact the tourist office.

▶ *Public phones in Frankfurt are usually card-operated*

Facilities for visitors with disabilities arriving at the city's main international airport are good, though travellers should inform their airlines in advance. For detailed information in English on these facilities download a brochure from Ⓦ www.frankfurt-airport.com

A useful source of advice when in Germany is **NatKo e.V.** ⓐ Kötherhofstr. 4, Mainz ⓣ (06131) 250 41

Useful websites include:
Ⓦ www.germany-tourism.de/ENG/infocenter/germany_for_disabled_travellers.htm
Ⓦ www.frankfurt-handicap.de (only in German)
Ⓦ www.sath.org (US-based site)
Ⓦ www.access-able.com (general advice on worldwide travel)
Ⓦ http://travel.guardian.co.uk/disabled for useful tips and links

TOURIST INFORMATION

Frankfurt Tourist Information ⓐ Hauptbahnhof, Eingangshalle (main railway station entrance) ⓣ (069) 2123 8800 Ⓦ www.frankfurt-tourismus.de Ⓛ 08.00–21.00 Mon–Fri, 09.00–18.00 Sat & Sun

Frankfurt Tourist Information Römer ⓐ Auf dem Römerberg ⓣ (069) 2123 8800 Ⓛ 09.30–17.30 Mon–Fri, 10.00–16.00 Sat & Sun

DZT (Central German Tourist Office), for general information on holidays in Germany. ⓐ Beethovenstr. 69, 60325 Frankfurt am Main ⓣ (069) 974 640 Ⓦ www.deutschland-tourismus.de

Hessen Touristik Service e.V. General information on Frankfurt's state of Hesse. ❷ Abraham-Lincoln-Str. 38–42, 65189 Wiesbaden ❶ (0611) 778 800 ⓦ www.hessen-tourismus.de

For local tourist offices outside Frankfurt see the relevant sections.

BACKGROUND READING

Happy Birthday, Turk by Jakob Arjouni. A crime novel set in Frankfurt during the 80s, with a hero reminiscent of Sam Spade and Philip Marlowe.

House of Rothschild: Money's Prophets: 1798–1848 by Niall Ferguson. A history of the Rothschilds, the Frankfurt family that dominated the European banking world in the 19th century.

Emergencies

The following are emergency free-call numbers:
Ambulance or emergency doctor (*Notarzt*) ☎ 112
Fire (*Feuerwehr*) ☎ 112
Police (*Polizei*) ☎ 110
In Frankfurt, there is also a 24hr emergency doctor service ☎ 19 292

MEDICAL SERVICES

If you need a doctor or dentist, check the local phone book under *Ärtzte* (doctors) or *Zahnärzte* (dentists). Otherwise ask at the local tourist office or contact your nearest embassy or consulate. The latter usually have lists of English-speaking doctors and dentists, and can also offer assistance in case of emergencies. Surgery hours are usually 09.00–12.00, 16.00–18.00 Mon–Fri, closed Wed afternoon, Sat & Sun.

Some English-speaking doctors (general practice)
Dr Prister ⓐ Zeil 111 ☎ (069) 231 860 Ⓦ www.prister.de
Dr Leo Najman ⓐ Schweizerstr. 5 ☎ (069) 616 707

Apothekennotdienst **(Emergency pharmacy)**
Information on after-hours emergency and weekend services is displayed in front of every pharmacy. Addresses are also listed in local papers and on the internet at Ⓦ www.frankfurt.de

Krankenhäuser **(Hospitals)**
Bethanien Krankenhaus ⓐ Im Prüfling 21–25 ☎ (069) 46 080
Hospital zum Heiligen Geist ⓐ Lange Str. 4–6 ☎ (069) 21 960
Krankenhaus Sachsenhausen ⓐ Schulstr. 31 ☎ (069) 66 050

Nordwest Krankenhaus ❸ Steinbacher Hohl 2–26 ❶ (069) 76 011
Rotes Kreuz Krankenhaus ❸ Königswarterstr. 16 ❶ (069) 40 710
St Katharinen Krankenhaus ❸ Seckbacher Landstr. 65 ❶ (069) 46 030
Städt Krankenhaus Höchst ❸ Gotenstr. 6–8, Höchst ❶ (069) 31 060
Universitätskliniken ❸ Theodor-Stern-Kai 7 ❶ (069) 63 011

Zahnärztlicher Notdienst **(Emergency dental service)**
❸ Universitätsklinikum Frankfurt Theodor-Stern-Kai 7
❶ (069) 6301 6713 or (069) 6301 5877

◔ *German pharmacies also advise on and treat minor ailments*

POLICE

Polizeipräsidium Frankfurt (Police headquarters) ⓐ Adickesallee 70
ⓣ (069) 75 500
Polizei Innenstadt (Inner city) ⓐ Zeil 33 ⓣ (069) 7551 0100

LOST PROPERTY

Fundbüro (Lost Property Office) ⓐ Erdgeschoss (ground floor),
Zimmer (rooms) 2–5, Mainzer Landstr. 315–321 ⓣ (069) 2124 2403 or
(069) 2124 2504 ⓛ 07.30–12.30 Mon, 07.30–12.30 Wed, 13.00–18.00
Thur, 07.30–12.30 Fri ⓢ S-Bahn: 3–5 to Galluswarte, then tram: 11 to
Schwalbacher Str. (direction Höchst)

EMBASSIES & CONSULATES

Australian Consulate-General ⓐ Grüneburgweg 58–62
ⓣ (069) 905 580 ⓦ www.germany.embassy.gov.au
ⓛ 08.30–13.00, 14.00–16.00 Mon–Thur, 08.30–15.30 Fri

EMERGENCY PHRASES

Help!	**Fire!**	**Stop!**
Hilfe!	Feuer!	Halt!
Heelfe!	*Foyer!*	*Halt!*

Call an ambulance/a doctor/the police/the fire service!
Rufen Sie bitte einen Krankenwagen/einen Arzt/die Polizei/
die Feuerwehr!
*Roofen zee bitter inen krankenvaagen/inen artst/dee politsye/
dee foyervair!*

British Consulate-General @ Yorckstrasse 19, Düsseldorf
📞 (0211) 94 480 🌐 www.britischebotschaft.de

Canadian Embassy @ Leipziger Platz 17, Berlin 📞 (030) 2031 2470;
Emergency line – toll free 00 800 2326 6831 🌐 www.dfait-
maeci.gc.ca/canada-europa/germany 🕐 09.00–12.00 Mon–Fri

New Zealand Embassy @ Friedrichstr. 60, 10117 Berlin 📞 (030) 206 210
🌐 www.nzembassy.com 🕐 09.00–13.00, 14.00–17.30 Mon–Thur,
09.00–13.00, 14.00–16.30 Fri

Republic of Ireland @ Friedrichstr. 200, Berlin 📞 (030) 220 720
🕐 9.30–12.30 Mon–Fri

Republic of South Africa @ Tiergartenstr. 18, Berlin 📞 (030) 2207 3202
🌐 www.suedafrika.org 🕐 09.00–12.00 Mon–Fri

US Consulate-General @ Giessener Str. 30 📞 (069) 75 350 (also after-
hours emergencies); American Citizen Services (069) 7535 2280
🌐 http://frankfurt.usconsulate.gov 🕐 08.00–12.00 Mon–Fri,
closed on American and German holidays.

WHAT'S IN YOUR GUIDEBOOK?

Independent authors Impartial up-to-date information from our travel experts who meticulously source local knowledge.

Experience Thomas Cook's 165 years in the travel industry and guidebook publishing enriches every word with expertise you can trust.

Travel know-how Contributions by thousands of staff around the globe, each one living and breathing travel.

Editors Travel-publishing professionals, pulling everything together to craft a perfect blend of words, pictures, maps and design.

You, the traveller We deliver a practical, no-nonsense approach to information, geared to how you really use it.

SPOT A CITY IN SECONDS

This great range of pocket city guides will have you in the know in no time. Lightweight and packed with detail on the most important things from shopping and sights to non-stop nightlife, they knock spots off chunkier, clunkier versions. Titles include:

Editorial/project management: Lisa Plumridge
Copy editor: Monica Guy
Layout/DTP: Pat Hinsley & Alison Rayner
Proofreader: Wendy Janes

The publishers would like to thank the following individuals and organisations for supplying their copyright photographs for this book: Andi Phaser Braun, page 13; Andrew Chambers ©istockphoto.com, page 17; Bristol Hotel, page 37; Claudia Dewald ©istockphoto.com, page 21; J. Kratschmer/Primus-Linie, page 80–1; Palmengarten der Stadt Frankfurt am Main, page 8; Steigenberger Frankfurter Hof, page 39; Tanja Schäfer/PIA Stadt Frankfurt am Main, page 40–1; Grant Bourne, all other pages.

Send your thoughts to
books@thomascook.com

- **Found a great bar, club, shop or must-see sight that we don't feature?**
- **Like to tip us off about any information that needs a little updating?**
- **Want to tell us what you love about this handy little guidebook and more importantly how we can make it even handier?**

Then here's your chance to tell all! Send us ideas, discoveries and recommendations today and then look out for your valuable input in the next edition of this title.

Email the above address (stating the title) or write to: CitySpots Project Editor, Thomas Cook Publishing, PO Box 227, Coningsby Road, Peterborough PE3 8SB, UK.